the Jesus Touch

LEARNING THE art of relationship
FROM THE master

the JESUS *Touch*

FOREWORD BY MAX LUCADO
LYNN ANDERSON

HOWARD
PUBLISHING CO.

Our purpose at Howard Publishing is to:
- *Increase faith* in the hearts of growing Christians
- *Inspire holiness* in the lives of believers
- *Instill hope* in the hearts of struggling people everywhere

Because He's coming again!

The Jesus Touch: Learning the Art of Relationship from the Master
© 2002 by Lynn Anderson
Revised and updated from the previously published *Heaven Came Down*
All rights reserved. Printed in the United States of America

Published by Howard Publishing Co., Inc.
3117 North 7th Street, West Monroe, Louisiana 71291-2227

02 03 04 05 06 07 08 09 10 11   10 9 8 7 6 5 4 3 2 1

Edited by Philis Boultinghouse
Interior Design by John Luke

ISBN: 1-58229-237-X

contents

FOREWORD
by Max Lucado

If you are task-driven but long to be people-oriented…

if you want to see people more as an opportunity than a burden…

if you can't see how the law of God works with the love of God…

if you catch yourself growing irritable at crowds, grumpy at inefficiency, or aggravated at ineptness…

then you are holding the right book.

Lynn Anderson has some words for your heart. He will do more than help you deal with people—he will help you love people. His model? The source of love himself: Jesus of Nazareth.

Read on and learn how Jesus dealt with difficult people.

ACKNOWLEDGMENTS

Long years have passed between the conception and the birth of this book. The "thought-trails" expressed in these pages can be traced at least as far back as the 1970s, when I fell into my first attempts to mentor college students in people skills. With time, the core concepts gathered layers of insight, picked up from dozens of sources that only God knows, as I taught "people-sensitivity" seminars across the country. Some ideas may actually be original with me—but for the life of me I don't know which ones. Some came from longtime colleagues, with special acknowledgments to Doug Kostowsky, Landon Saunders, Stanley Shipp, David Lewis, and David Wray. Some came from the writings of such scholars as the late Donald G. Miller, John Stott, and others.

Some of my former students have taught my material in more than a dozen countries around the globe and have then contributed to the material as well. Among these ex-students is Max Lucado. Many years ago, while in Miami and later in Rio de Janeiro, Max taught this material many times, adding to and adjusting it. While Max was in Brazil, he and I began to collaborate on this book. Max roughed out the first draft from cassettes of sessions I had taught. Then we shuffled manuscripts between Brazil and the U.S. awhile. Busy schedules finally stalled the project, and the embryonic manuscript lay in my files for several years.

A publishing deadline finally revived the manuscript. I have reworked and updated the material, adding more chapters to bring it to its final form, but if some of this sounds like a young Max Lucado—it is.

To Max and to all who influenced this book, I am deeply indebted. Many thanks as well to Lyn Rose and Judy Bowyer for grueling hours of typing and to Philis Boultinghouse for the editorial magic that made the final product ready for print.

I pray that Jesus will shine through and leave his mark on those who read it.

WHAT? ME, insensitive?

IT CAN BE CURED

Carolyn and I sat aboard an aircraft in Victoria, British Columbia, ready for departure. From our little oval window, we spotted several luggage wagons parked on the tarmac—all piled high with magazines. Then we noticed that every one of those hundreds of magazines bore the same name: *People* magazine. All over America, millions of people would soon slap down three dollars a throw just to read about the goings on of other human beings! Amazing, considering that most of us get our fill of people every day.

It set us to thinking: The only real difference between *People* magazine and most other magazines sold today is the name! Most magazines are about people. *Life* magazine is about people; *Sports Illustrated* is about people; *Time, Newsweek, Popular Mechanics,* even *The Wall Street Journal* are about people. This shouts something about human nature. We people are enormously fascinated with each other. The radio plays songs that are primarily about people; TV is mostly pictures of people. At the movies, we pay good money to sit in the dark and watch two-dimensional pictures of imaginary people. We read novels to get inside the psyches of people. Sometimes, for recreation, we go to the mall to people watch. Even daily conversation is mostly about people. We are driven by our *passion for people.* In fact, our fascination with people is one of the ways in which we are like God.

Since we people are so intrinsically interested in people, when we focus instead on things, ideas, tasks, status, or institutions, we do serious damage to the central matrix of our humanity—not to mention the damage we do to people around us. A coworker drove this home to me in a very personal way a few years back.

This coworker had been in our office only a few weeks, but something wasn't working right. So I sat down to chat with her a minute, hoping to help her work through *her* problem. "Something seems to be bothering you. Can I help?"

I wasn't quite prepared for what I heard next.

"You are plastic!" she said for openers. "You want this church to be user-friendly and open, but *you* aren't. You are inaccessible and insensitive. You constantly break appointments because you're 'too busy' with what *you* want to do. And you are making the people in this office feel like peons. You are supposed to be a spiritual leader, but I see you as completely unapproachable."

I was stunned. Me? Unapproachable? Insensitive? Surely not me! I tried to deny her accusations, rationalize them, and blame everybody else. But…really, she was dead right. There was nothing to do but to face my insensitivity, own it, and apologize to her and one by one to the whole staff. And then I began the task of getting back on track.

Yet how had this happened? Didn't I have a reputation for being warm, approachable, and people-oriented? Hadn't I built a long and visible track record of good relationships?

But this painful moment of truth forced me to look honestly at the past many months. Everything was a blur. My pocket calendar was as cluttered as a city dump. Far too many speaking engagements. Way too much travel. Two new books. A new church. Helping launch a new journal. Teaching a graduate course. And page after page of appointments moved or canceled. The pace had gradually accelerated, reaching an all-time high over the last few weeks as I was fighting the contract deadline, ironically, on this book, *The Jesus Touch: Learning the Art of Relationship from the Master*! And as my internal engines exceeded the redline, I had become less and less available, more and more self-absorbed.

I am a people person, but I had allowed myself to become task-driven. For months I had not only been neglecting people, but I'd been leaving hurt and disillusioned bodies in my wake, jeopardizing the very things I really believe are most important. Because my life was not people-sensitive, it was drifting toward disaster.

God's number-one priority is people. To do his main thing, God became "a people" and moved to live among people. Jesus, who became God in a body, was out there on the people turf. For Jesus, people are job one. For authentic followers of Jesus, people become top priority as well.

The Bible says that when Jesus owns us and fills us, we see people in a whole new way. "For Christ's love compels us" and thus we "should no longer live for [ourselves], but for him…. So from now on *we regard no one from a worldly point of view."* We have a new view of people because "if anyone is in Christ, he is a new creation; the old has gone, the new has come!" (2 Cor. 5:14–17). The old view of people is gone! The new view of people has come. And since we are "Christ's ambassadors," God is "making his appeal through us" (v. 20). So God, who is in the people business, has also called us to people-centered living. Thus, the most godlike thing we can do is to treat people like Jesus did.

From Abstract to Concrete

When the crowds asked Jesus, "What is the greatest command-ment?" he answered, "Love the Lord your God with all your soul, with all your mind and with all your strength." That raised no eye-brows and rocked no boats. It was merely the familiar ancient *Shema,* which ended all synagogue meetings. By the time good Jewish boys grew beards, they had quoted the *Shema* a thousand times.

"Good boy, Jesus. Good answer," the crowd would have nodded in agreement. It was comfortably abstract. And as long as loving God is an abstraction aimed at no target in particular, we are all OK. Ho-hum religion. Business as usual.

But then Jesus *added* a line. "Love your neighbor as yourself" (Mark 12:31). Oops! Things changed. Hackles went up. Now, wait a minute. Everything was fine like it was. "Love God" has a nice ring to it. Sounds religious. And it can be kept comfortably abstract.

But that added line from Jesus dispelled the vagueness and slammed the abstract down onto the concrete. Now Jesus had gone and targeted that teaching. He'd made it practical. He'd aimed it at real people.

As long as loving God is one of those vague abstractions, we are all OK. We can put on and take off our religion like we do our Sunday clothes. We can set our faith up on the shelf beside our dusty family Bible and still feel holy. But when Jesus targeted that teaching, well, things got practical and personal.

The way Jesus put it, our love for God is expressed, not in pews, pulpits, and stained-glass tones, but in relationships with people—in the way you and I get along with him and her and them. If being with God on Sunday doesn't make us better at being with people on Monday, then we've missed the point. Real religion shines in right relationships.

The grist of Christianity is ground out in the mill of marriages, friendships, partnerships, neighborhoods, communities, property lines, and sales contracts. Or to simplify it, if we really love God, the first ones to benefit will be family, friends, and neighbors.

Hmm. That complicates things a bit, especially when you think about our neighbors! Grumpy ones. Mean ones. Lazy ones. Bosses who demand the impossible. Secretaries who can't perform the minimal. Wives who don't appreciate what wonderful husbands they have. Husbands who think they are too wonderful. Relating to people with "the Jesus touch" is easier said than done. As the old saying goes,

> To live above with those we love,
> O, how that will be glory.
> But to live below with those we know,
> Is quite a different story.

How Are Your Relationships?

We come into the world in families. Then we must fit into society, schools, and other organizations. And as Stephen Covey says, "We must interact with others for success to come to us in any personally effective way." Covey cites a study conducted by the Carnegie Institute that found that 60 to 80 percent of job dismissals in the business industry are caused by social problems, and only 20 to 40 percent are due to technical incompetence. In other words, most firings were because of relationship trouble. This study showed that in the field of engineering, only 15 percent of one's success is due to technical knowledge; the other 85 percent is due to one's ability to get along with other people.[1]

What does all this mean? It means that not merely your success, but also your personal fulfillment—maybe even your survival—depend on your ability to manage and nurture healthy relationships.

But it sure is hard for us to get along with each other. Linus, the Peanuts comic strip character, said it for all of us: "I love the world. It's *people* I can't stand." Doing right by people is the Christian's forte. Isn't our mission the same as Jesus'? Touching people? Didn't John say, "For anyone who does not love his brother, whom he has seen, cannot love God, whom he has not seen"? (1 John 4:20).

So we come to an important personal question: *How are your relationships?* Think for just a minute about the people in your world. Some are in your life by choice: your mate, your best friend, perhaps a business associate. Others you inherited by chance: your relatives, your next-door neighbor, maybe your boss. But no matter how you became connected with them, they all have one thing in common: They are vulnerable and woundable people who need someone to love them unreservedly—just like you and I do!

Could you use a little help in doing right by people? I guess we all could.

That, in a nutshell, is the purpose of this book: to coach you on how to treat the people that God has put in your world. The plan? Simple. Jesus will be our coach. We will track down the way Jesus treated people, and we'll learn the art of relationship from the Master. And no one marks the way more clearly than the apostle John.

Why John?

Why John? Several reasons. First, no one in Scripture walked more intimately with Jesus. In some special way, John was "that disciple Jesus loved." And no New Testament disciple walked with Jesus longer than had the aged apostle John by the time this Gospel was written.

Second, John wrote his gospel several decades after the other gospels were written. By the time he wrote it, the church had already begun to form some of the crust of institutionalism. When movements begin, they are flexible and fluid; then they gradually form structure and tradition, which serve to stabilize them. But this structure and tradition also tend to immobilize and desensitize them.

And, worst of all, institutionalized religion tends to become less people-sensitive. In fact, religious institutions can end up crushing people, even those people who are most Christian. This kind of institutional immobility was already slowing the Christian movement before John died. Some bishops were becoming dictatorial. Organizational structures were growing more complex. Mini-denominations were taking shape. Policies, creeds, and doctrinal statements loomed on the horizon.

The Christ-follower movement was losing people-sensitivity too. And in the midst of all this sat sensitive Saint John, now nearly a century old. Perhaps John's hair shone silver and his health was dwindling to frail. All his fellow apostles had long since gone on. Peter, James, and Andrew had been called home. No doubt he felt alone as he faced the changing times.

The aged apostle had witnessed the launching of this movement. Now he saw it languishing.

As John watched the Christian movement institutionalize and lose freshness and people-focus, his mind may have wandered back to the way things were in the beginning. So spontaneous. So flexible. So full of energy, so relationship-oriented and people-sensitive. Why, the very core of Jesus' work had been a three-year relationship with twelve close friends.

Surely John remembered the Messiah at the wedding who solved the wine problem and got the host off the hook. John thought of the blind beggar whom no one noticed except Jesus. He pondered Jesus' tender teaching of the Samaritan woman and his tough, direct encounter with Nicodemus. He saw Jesus' tears as he embraced Mary and Martha, consoling them in the loss of their brother Lazarus.

Third, the old apostle also knew that just as institutions become desensitized, so a crust could form around the heart of an individual believer. Relationships can give way to religion, and a Christian can lose his or her "first love."

One can almost hear John thinking aloud. "Jesus was so tender with people, yet so tough with issues. *Jesus and people.* That is it!" And John remembered.

So John wrote it down. "These [things] are written that you may believe that Jesus is the Christ, the Son of God, and that by believing you may have life in his name" (John 20:31). In other words, "I want to build your faith!" In the Gospel of John, "faith" is always a verb; it is never a noun. Faith is about how you live, not just about what you think is true. Mostly, "verb-faith" in Jesus is about touching and building people the way Jesus touched them. So John packaged his high-powered, faith-building theology in human-interest stories. Stories about people. Stories about relationships. Ordinary encounter after ordinary encounter. Each vignette carefully selected to weave a tapestry of ageless wisdom. Heaven reaching down to humanity, Immanuel among earthlings, the Christ amidst the commoners, *Jesus touching people.*

With graphic detail and penetrating insight, John takes us on a storybook journey through Jesus' encounters with human beings. All kinds of people:

- religious people like Nicodemus

- self-righteous people like some Pharisees

- abandoned people like the woman at the well

- frightened people like the woman caught in adultery

- despairing people like Mary and Martha at the tomb of Lazarus

- lonely people like the handicapped man by the pool

- mistreated people like the blind beggar by the road

And the common thread that strings all these souls together is their basic humanity. They had flesh and bones, problems and joys, friends and enemies—just like you and me!

They could have been your neighbors or your relatives. That cranky old coot who lives around the corner? He is in John's story. That group of church officials who can't see God? Jesus ran into a few of those. Your mother-in-law? The pregnant teenager? The grief-stricken widow? You'll see their faces in the pages of John's writings. And what's more, Jesus is one of them; yet in him you'll see God act out his own commandment: You'll watch him love them as he loved himself, and you'll want to love like that!

You will also observe divine people skills, and you can learn them. You will see that God does his most awesome work through relationships. Hopefully, with a touch from beyond, your own relationships will be changed!

At a baptismal service, one of our friends was explaining the significance of what she was witnessing to her three-year-old daughter. "See that lady?" the mother asked. "Jesus is about to wash away her sins."

The little girl sat up a bit straighter so she could see better and said with excitement, "Good, I've been wanting to see Jesus."

Me, too, little one. Me, too!

Maybe you have too. Maybe you have heard Jesus' words about loving your neighbor as yourself and have thought, *I'd like to see what he would do with that in my world!* Well, now is your chance. Open your heart a bit, and let John teach you how Jesus touched people.

Chapter 1

STREET-LEVEL messiah

OF LOVERS AND USERS

When the desert preacher, John, pointed his bony finger and exploded, "That's him!" we couldn't believe our eyes. Goodness knows we had heard enough about him. He was all John talked about. But we'd actually begun to wonder if the desert preacher really knew. Then rumors about him roamed the countryside. Strange things. Lights moving through the sky. Otherworldly choir music out in the country at night. Disturbing ideas. Miracles!

Now here he was on our street. You could have knocked me over with a feather when John spotted him in the next block, headed our way. We watched bug-eyed and held our breath while he walked by. My pulse raced. Yet frankly, part of me was…a bit disappointed. He was so ordinary. If John hadn't said something, I would never have picked him out of the crowd. He looked pretty much like any other Galilean carpenter, except maybe for his eyes—the way he looked at us.

James and I let him get a few strides past us, then we fell in behind him. I'm not sure why. It seems sort of dumb now as I look back. But, somehow, we couldn't resist him. I guess we both hoped he might notice us, and at the same time were afraid he would. Then, without warning, he turned around and spoke to us. I was so rattled that I didn't really hear what he said. James told me later that he'd asked us a simple question: "You fellows looking for something?"

Where my next line came from, I'll never know, but I stammered back, "Uh...where do you live?" Silly question. But it was all I could come up with. Yet, somehow, the way he answered made me feel as if it was the most appropriate question in the world—as if God had planned for centuries that I should ask exactly that.

Then his eyes twinkled with a warm light, and he said, "Come and see."

We followed him home that day...been following ever since.

John saw Jesus coming toward him and said, "Look, the Lamb of God, who takes away the sin of the world! This is the one I meant when I said, 'A man who comes after me has surpassed me because he was before me.' I myself did not know him, but the reason I came baptizing with water was that he might be revealed to Israel."

The next day John was there again with two of his disciples. When he saw Jesus passing by, he said, "Look, the Lamb of God!"

When the two disciples heard him say this, they followed Jesus. Turning around, Jesus saw them following and asked, "What do you want?"

They said, "Rabbi" (which means Teacher), "where are you staying?"

"Come," he replied, "and you will see."

So they went and saw where he was staying, and spent that day with him.

John 1:29, 35–39

STREET-LEVEL messiah

OF LOVERS AND USERS

Four principles. Like four legs on a chair—a balanced place to rest one's convictions. Like four walls in a room—a shelter from the chill of cold people and a shadow from the blistering heat of hotheads. Four solid traits. Four tools found in the Master's tool chest for building relationships with people.

Over and over these four principles weave their way in and out of the Gospels, creating a tapestry of four colors. Each blending with the other, each creating the other, each supporting the other.

Yet each one unique. They are common in purpose, but different in function. Alone, each helps us, but together, they transform us. They were designed in heaven for use on earth. Four basic "people principles." They frame the Jesus touch:

- Jesus was *available* to people.

- Jesus was *sensitive* to people.

- Jesus was *helpful* to people.

- Jesus was *creative* in his connection with each unique person.

Available

Let's take it from the top. Principle number one: Jesus was *available* to people. John makes this clear up front. "The Word became flesh and made his dwelling *among* us" (John 1:14). He was with God, he was God, and he made everything; yet he became flesh. He pitched his tent right smack in the middle of our campground; he rented a house on your block and walked down my street.

> IF I AM GOING TO FOLLOW JESUS' LEAD, I WILL BE AVAILABLE TO PEOPLE.

Let's walk with Jesus into his first conversation in the Gospel of John. A young prophet and a few of his friends were standing in an ancient village street. "John [the Baptist] saw *Jesus coming toward him*" (John 1:29). That's street-level availability. There was Jesus, on the street, walking toward John the Baptizer and two of John's friends. He was *physically* accessible.

For some reason, the two disciples fell in behind Jesus and followed him. Sensing them behind him, Jesus turned on his heel and asked, "What do you want?"

Apparently caught off-guard, they fielded his question with one of their own: "Where are you staying?"

"Come," he replied, "and you will see." So they went and saw where he was staying, and they spent the day with him. Jesus wasn't hiding out somewhere in an office, running a rigid schedule that allowed no time for people. He was with the people. In this instance he made his whole day available to these seekers. (I wish I knew what he knows without having to hide in the office to learn it.) What's more, Jesus wasn't merely physically present, he was *personally* approachable and *emotionally* accessible to people as well. He was approachable. People seemed to feel comfortable just walking up and talking to him, asking him questions, carrying on a conversation. Sometimes when he was teaching his disciples, they even interrupted him in the middle of his sermons, and he didn't seem to mind at all. In fact, that seemed to be how he wanted it.

What are the implications for me? Obviously, if I am going to follow Jesus' lead, I will be available to people. I need to be where the people are. And not just physically near, but personally and emotionally approachable. As my coworker so courageously but kindly pointed out to me, there is something both askew and less than credible about a person who professes to be spiritually alive but is physically, personally, and emotionally unapproachable. Amen and ouch!

Sensitive

Principle number two: Jesus was *sensitive.* He was tuned in. He picked up on subtle "people-signals." John noticed this early in his Gospel. Watch as the desert prophet pointed out Jesus walking down the street and how the prophet's disciples fell in behind Jesus. What does a person do when he suddenly notices a couple of people following him? He either quickens his pace or turns and confronts. Right? Jesus turned and faced these curious followers. But not so much to confront as to engage them in a friendly dialogue.

He sensed someone following him, yes. He wasn't hidden away in his own contemplative ivory tower. He walked in the real world, aware of the people around him. But on an even deeper level, Jesus sensed some of *why* they were following. When Jesus turned, he perceptively inquired, "What do you want?" or was it, "What can I do for you?"

When you are following someone who suddenly wheels around

and speaks to you, you somehow feel obligated to explain what you are up to, right? And likely, at first, you will be at a loss for words. Seems the disciples were too. They responded, "Uh…uh…where do you live?" What else could they say? Jesus, still sensitive—first to their quest and now their feelings of awkwardness—replied, "Come and see." He could have squelched their "Where do you live?" with "That's a dumb question. I don't live anyplace. Foxes have holes, birds have nests. But I don't have a place to lay my head." Rather, he gently invited, "Come and see."

Jesus wasn't saying, "I'm over at the Hilton, room 326. Come and look at the place." No, I think Jesus meant, "Come with me, and I will show you something about the perspective from which I live my life. Come, and I'll show you the wonderful world of the spirit."

Jesus was always sensitive. Later in the same chapter of John's gospel, Jesus introduced Nathaniel: "Here's a true Israelite, in whom there is nothing false."

"How do you know me?" Nathaniel asked.

"When you were over there under the fig tree," Jesus explained, "before Philip even called you, *I saw you*" (see John 1:47–48). More than mechanics is conveyed here. Jesus doesn't merely mean, "A beam of light struck you and bounced onto my optic nerve, transferring your image to my brain." Rather, Jesus *perceived* something about Nathaniel. Jesus is sensitive. This leaves me asking, "Am I the kind of person who picks up on the subtle signals people send?" If not, why? Honestly, why not? And if I do, why?

The Difference between Lovers and Users

After all, two very different kinds of characters are people-sensitive: the lovers and the users. Some people have become skilled at reading subtle people-signals because they are lovers. They care about people, so they study people all the time. Love sharpens our people-sensitive skills.

Users also become sensitive to people-signals—but for a very different purpose. Some hawkers at circus sideshows can read people like a book. They know how to manipulate people. Fortunetellers ask leading questions, probing here and there; they pick up on clothing, facial expression, and body language. They are sensitive to people, all right. But they are people sensitive because they're users.

Of course, Jesus was a *lover*, not a *user!* His followers are to be skillful lovers as well. This means being alert to the environment and keeping your head in the game. Someone has said, "If you are not completely where you are, wherever you are, then you are nowhere."

Sharpening Our People-Sensitivity

While the Spirit within us is the fountain source of people-sensitivity ("God has poured out his love into our hearts by the Holy Spirit" [Rom. 5:5]), we can help each other learn sensitivity as well. Especially, parents can help children. When our children were small, Carolyn and I defined five qualities we wanted to nurture in our kids.

First, and foremost, we wanted them to love God.

Second, we wanted them to develop a healthy self-esteem; third, to be self-starters; fourth, to manage healthy relationships. Finally, we wanted our children to be people-sensitive. We tried our best to model people-sensitivity before them. But we also tried all sorts of other strategies to people-sensitize our kids. One effective little strategy was a game we played with them in parks, malls, airports, or any other good place for people-watching. We would pick out some interesting passerby and challenge the kids to make up a story about that person.

But they had to give reasons why their story could be true. "That man over there is very lonely. He looks sad. Last night while he was sleeping alone on a park bench, he..."

"Why do you think he slept on a park bench?"

"Because his clothes are wrinkled, he looks poor, and he needs a shave. And you can smell that he didn't get a shower this morning...."

The kids would go on watching for clues, making up stories about strangers, and in so doing, sharpening their powers of observation, deepening their hearts, and refining their people-sensitivity. We believe God blessed those games.

Helpful

Principle number three: Jesus was *helpful.* Some folks are only superficially available and sensitive, but not helpful at all. Bleeding hearts.

They wring their hands and whine, "Ain't it awful, what's happening to so-and-so?" Or, "Oh, I feel so deeply for people that I just can't stand to go into a hospital room because I get sick myself out of empathy." Or, "I can't comfort the bereaved because my sensitivity to grief absolutely devastates me." That's not *people*-sensitivity! That's *self*-sensitivity. People-sensitive people look for ways to help. Self-sensitive people duck unpleasant experiences, even if it means neglecting the sick or the brokenhearted! Truly sensitive people pay the cost of getting involved. You'd think everyone would naturally be helpful. But not always.

Just ask Eleanor Bradley. While shopping on Fifth Avenue in crowded Manhattan, she fell and broke her leg. She sat helpless, crying and calling for someone to be kind enough to help her. How long would you guess she cried? Two minutes? Ten minutes? Twenty minutes? Keep guessing. This woman pleaded for *forty* minutes as people walked on by before someone stopped and actually helped her!

If we could interview those who walked around and stepped over Eleanor Bradley, we might be surprised. Would some be civic leaders? Businesspeople? Would some be Christians? How am I on the helpfulness chart? How is your track record of kindness? Let's think about it: Is there someone in your path who could use your help right now?

- that colleague at work who has more assignments than he can possibly get done

- that young mother down the street whose day is framed with baby food and diapers

- the teenager who has no parent to pick him or her up after school

- the elderly woman who may need a strong back to help her move some furniture

Helpfulness is the "bread and butter" of the Christian virtues. It is to be "standard equipment" on all models. Not all can preach. Few can lead. Not everyone is a musician or can counsel or teach. But *all* can be helpful. Anyone can roll up his or her pants legs and wade into the flood of day-to-day hassles and hurts of others. And to do this is to do what Jesus did; it is, in fact, to be like God! It is the Jesus touch.

Now look back at Jesus! The first question he asked those two guys who were soft-shoeing furtively along behind him was, "What do you seek?" Read: "What can I do for you? Is there something I can do to help?" Jesus' question was not a challenge, "What are you guys after?" but helpful empathy, "Is there something I can help you with?"

"Yes, there is," they said. "We want to know where you live."

He said, "All right, fine, I can help you with that. Come with me, and I'll show you." Now, his agenda wasn't what they expected. But my, was he helpful. A helping person is a Jesus person.

Creative

Availability, sensitivity, and helpfulness. Quite a trio. But let's unveil the fourth and most exciting feature in Jesus' style! Jesus' touch was *creative*.

A friend pointed out that God has a thing about differentness and variety. Just one example: In a cubic foot of snow, there are eighteen million individual crystals, and no two of them have ever been found to be exactly alike. God only makes originals. He doesn't allow copies. He breaks every mold he uses. This creative genius reaches its crescendo in human beings. We are "fearfully and wonderfully made" (Ps. 139:14). God's grace is so multicolored that he cannot reflect himself in only one kind of human being.

Look away from this page for a moment. Examine the tips of your fingers. Use a magnifying glass if you need to, and study your fingerprints. Each fingerprint is unique. No two have been found alike. That's how the cops track down criminals. Yours are different from any other fingerprints in the whole wide world, maybe the only ones with your particular pattern that have ever existed. Or ever will exist. How wonderful! And the God who went to the trouble to design uniqueness on our fingertips didn't stop there. The God who makes one-of-a-kind fingerprints graciously puts them on the end of one-of-a-kind people, as well. Our uniqueness runs up our arms and into our whole bodies, throughout our emotional histories and into our priceless one-of-a-kind original souls! And since God has made each person uniquely different, Jesus creatively deals with every person in a fresh, unique way.

Start with a Question

Jesus did not use manipulative techniques on people. Nor should we, his followers. In fact, as we study Jesus and people, we are not looking for techniques. God himself in flesh stands in awe of the sacredness and dignity of human personality. He employs neither pressure tactics nor standardized techniques. He does not batter down the walls of people's resistance, nor does he bulldoze his way into the sanctity of their hearts. Instead, he approaches each unique person carefully—and very *creatively*.

The first "creative touch" of Jesus we observe is his *creative use of questions*. Follow him through his ministry, and you'll see that Jesus repeatedly asked questions. Jesus opened many of his encounters in the Gospel of John with a simple but creative question. Examples? "Will you give me a drink?" (John 4:7). "Do you want to get well?" (John 5:6). "You do not want to leave too, do you?" (John 6:67). "Do you believe in the Son of Man?" (John 9:35). "I am the resurrection and the life.... Do you believe this?" (John 11:25–26). Jesus begins relationships, grants dignity to people, and even opens up closed minds with simple questions.

> THE GOD WHO MAKES ONE-OF-A-KIND FINGERPRINTS GRACIOUSLY PUTS THEM ON THE END OF ONE-OF-A-KIND PEOPLE.

We religious types often seem more inclined toward *telling* than *asking*—even though most people like to be asked before they get told. For Jesus, people are just too valuable to simply "get told." He sees us as free and capable of doing our own responding. So he asked questions. *Asking* gives dignity to *people*. And Jesus allowed each person to think for him- or herself. Modern educators find this to be a sound educational principle. It's also a wonderful and welcomed conversational skill.

One day back in 1971, I boarded a plane and settled in beside a twenty-something young man who appeared noticeably nervous. Assuming he feared flying, I ventured, "You fly much?"

He assured me he was no "white-knuckle" novice, that he flew all the time. Then added, "Why do you ask?"

I explained, "You seemed a bit nervous, and I thought maybe…"

"No, no," he said, "That's not it at all. I am pretty nervous, all right. But it's because I'm on my way to Vietnam."

What would you say next? I lost my bearings but stumbled on, "Oh, uh, well, er, how long do you expect to be over there?"

A long silence preceded the next words. He stared out the window and said quietly, "I don't expect to come back."

His answer unnerved me. I waited a few nervous moments then probed, "Tell me about it."

"Three of my high school friends went over there, and they're never coming back. Not even in a box. Man, I really don't expect to come back alive either."

Tears welled up. Silence. Then I observed, "That's a tough thing to face. Do you have any idea how you're going to deal with all of that?"

"Oh, yeah," his face brightened.

I thought maybe he was a bright-eyed, bushy-tailed, born-again seminary student and was getting ready to lay his testimony on me. I leaned in.

"Well, I'm going to save up all my money so that just in case I ever do get back on American soil again, I'll be able to buy a brand-new purple motorcycle. I'll just live for that day!"

Four simple questions! Actually, four innocent but important questions. I had no strategy in mind when I asked them and was actually just making small talk. But those small questions not only opened up his universe and surfaced the terror buried in his soul, they also measured his flimsy resources for coping with such over-whelming possibilities. And I don't think he felt intruded upon at all.

On another occasion, I found myself in a bizarre conversation that could have gone a lot better with one or two well-placed questions. Carolyn and I sat by a hotel pool when an interesting couple walked by with their children in tow. A New Testament stuck out of the back pocket of the man's blue jeans, which were pulled down neatly over his cowboy boots and rolled up one turn at the bottom.

Something inside of me said, "This guy has got to be religious; he might even be clergy." So I engaged him in conversation. "Do you farm near here?"

"No," he explained stiffly, "I'm a gospel preacher."

Some strange quirk in my nature chose not to reveal who I was. So for nearly an hour I pretended to be an "evangelistic prospect." In fact, I never did tell him who I was or what I did—mostly because he never asked. In fact, he never asked me anything. He merely "told."

I inquired, "Oh, what kind of preacher is that?"

"Well, what kind is there? I preach Jesus, like in the New Testament."

"What is the New Testament?" Carolyn threw me a threatening glance, as she dived behind a newspaper!

"Second part of the Bible. First there is the Old Testament and then the New Testament."

"So you don't believe in the Old Testament?"

"Well, that's not exactly…"

He held forth awhile on dispensationalism and Hebrew versus Greek manuscripts, etc. I couldn't resist the temptation to push things further.

"At what seminary did you get your rabbi's degree?"

"I'm not a rabbi, I'm a Christian minister."

"What kind of church?"

"The kind that Jesus started on the day of Pentecost."

"The day of *what?*"

Carolyn glared at me over the corner of her newspaper.

"It was a Jewish holiday."

"Oh, so you *are* a Jewish preacher?"

Although he was very patient with me and was eager to answer my questions, he didn't seem even remotely interested in what I thought or in me as a person. He just led me on a survey of theology, church history, the plan of salvation, "true worship"—all orthodox Christianity, I suppose. However, if he had only asked one or two questions about me and really listened to my answers, the whole conversation would have been unnecessary.

If, on the other hand, I had been who this man thought I was, I would scarcely have understood a word he was saying. The incomprehensible, technical religious jargon would have dismantled any spiritual interest I might have brought to the conversation. And I certainly would not have connected any of his abstractions with my life.

The reason I remember this encounter so clearly is that I have been on his end of this conversation a thousand times. I feel pained when I think how many sincere people I may have turned off, not necessarily because my message was wrong, but because I started in the wrong place. I didn't ask enough of the right questions. I was more interested in telling than listening. How many may have tried to understand but simply couldn't decode my message? How many would love to know God if only they could peel away the layers of religious packaging I wrapped around him? How many felt regarded as "prospects" rather than as people? Oh yes, a few well-placed questions could have made all the difference!

Don't Be Intrusive

Questions must be carefully chosen and delicately worded, however, or they can be fists hammering on the doors of personal privacy. Have you ever been questioned rat-ta-tat-ta-tat style and felt as if someone were breaking and entering your psyche? You wanted to run. When Jesus touched John's disciples that day on the street, he did not cross-examine them. He never did. His questions are always sensitive, often indirect—people-oriented, not agenda-oriented.

> HOW MANY WOULD LOVE TO KNOW GOD IF ONLY THEY COULD PEEL AWAY THE LAYERS OF RELIGIOUS PACKAGING I WRAPPED AROUND HIM?

Nor were Jesus' questions manipulative like the kind salespeople sometimes use—cleverly sequenced so that whatever you answer, the sales rep will pick up on your response and lead you to another crossroads, where he nails you with another leading question. Several years ago when one salesman came to our house, Carolyn and I preplanned that no matter what he said, neither of us would say a word.

He walked in. I greeted him with a fixed smile. He spoke a few sentences then asked a question.

We just smiled at him. He waited. We kept smiling (and squirming). The salesman shifted directions, verbally walked us to another crossroads, then stopped and asked another leading question. We just kept smiling. After a half-dozen questions, the salesman gathered up his papers, threw them into his briefcase, and headed out the door muttering to himself.

I'm not suggesting that every salesperson is a manipulator. I am certainly not recommending the silent treatment for all hard-working salespeople. I'm saying that Jesus didn't use manipulative and intrusive questions. His questions were genuine-concern questions, the kind of respectful questions that pulled him up alongside people, gently opening hearts, yet allowing the comfort zone of the other person to dictate the pace.

The "Word became flesh and lived for a while among us," thus, we "have seen his glory," says John (see John 1:14). His glory was available. Sensitive. Helpful. Creative. Now Jesus has delegated the work of revealing God's nature in our world to us, his followers. Incredible! We are "Christ's ambassadors, as though God were making his appeal through us" (2 Cor. 5:20). So we become "God expressed in human form" on the street where we live. That means that we, his followers, must learn how to treat others as Jesus would treat them, creatively tailoring our approach to the wonderful uniqueness of each person. And here, in Jesus' encounter with the disciples of John, we find creative touch number one: *questions*. One godlike, people-sensitive quality is the art of gentle, well-chosen questions. Let's learn more. Turn the page and look for other creative Christlike keys to healthy human relationships.

Creative Touch

Ask gentle, well-chosen questions.

Thought Questions

1. Are you an approachable person? In what ways are you and what ways not?

2. What kinds of insights are necessary to be sensitive?

3. How would a person cultivate sensitivity and approachability?

Action Questions

1. Is there a person with needs who has been reaching out to you whom you have avoided? What specific step might you take next? What would Jesus do?

2. What gentle question might open or deepen your relationship with that person?

3. Experiment: In your next conversation with a friend, try asking thoughtful but not invasive questions. Then show your genuine interest by listening attentively to his or her answers. Follow up your friend's response with another thoughtful question.

Chapter 2

THE WINE OF kindness

HELPING A HOST OFF THE HOOK

Panic on the servants' faces signaled that something was going very wrong at my daughter's wedding. Then the maître d' whispered in my ear, "Master, we've run out of wine."

My mouth went dry, and my stomach knotted. My first thought was: *I've ruined the biggest day in the life of my sweet, trusting daughter.*

Then I realized I may have even ruined myself! Everyone knows that a wedding invitation for distant travelers implies that I will provide everything for them—lodging and food, music and dancing—and, of course, wine. Our courts actually regard such an invitation as a legal contract. Why, rumor has it that when Ben Enoch over in Capernaum ran out of wine at his daughter's wedding, poor Ben was hit with a half-dozen lawsuits—destroyed him financially.

I couldn't figure out why I was running out of wine. Then I saw that country carpenter talking to my servants. Maybe he and his twelve tagalongs were drinking more than their share. Look, his mother is whispering something to him; I hope it's a tongue-lashing on protocol.

22

The nerve of that guy! Wait a minute. Would you believe...?

Well, young John may have told you what happened next. Oh yes, it's true. But given who he claims to be, it's the last thing I would have expected. Surely he might have done something...well...something more godlike! Maybe chided me for carelessness or even stepped up on the table and delivered a scorching sermon on "Wine is a mocker." But, no. It seems my feelings mattered to him more than my blunders.

I agree with his twelve friends. They said they saw God's glory that day. The glory of God the miraculous winemaker? No! Real glory! The glory of a God who begins with our feelings rather than our failures, a God who cares more about our hearts than our history. Who besides God?

"Dear woman, why do you involve me?" Jesus replied. "My time has not yet come."

His mother said to the servants, "Do whatever he tells you."

Nearby stood six stone water jars, the kind used by the Jews for ceremonial washing, each holding from twenty to thirty gallons.

Jesus said to the servants, "Fill the jars with water"; so they filled them to the brim.

Then he told them, "Now draw some out and take it to the master of the banquet."

They did so, and the master of the banquet tasted the water that had been turned into wine. He did not realize where it had come from, though the servants who had drawn the water knew. Then he called the bridegroom aside and said, "Everyone brings out the choice wine first and then the cheaper wine after the guests have had too much to drink; but you have saved the best till now."

This, the first of his miraculous signs, Jesus performed at Cana in Galilee. He thus revealed his glory, and his disciples put their faith in him.

John 2:4–11

Chapter 2

THE WINE OF kindness

HELPING A HOST OFF THE HOOK

The plot seems too simple. Jesus and his disciples visit a wedding. The host runs out of wine. Apparently, the wine shop is closed. So Jesus, at his mother's urging, turns six jugs of water into six jugs of wine! Simple, huh? But what is this story doing in the Bible? The conclusion seems so open-ended. And, without question, this one little vignette has triggered a thousand arguments over wine drinking and Christian temperance. Where is the meat here? The action? The depth?

This water-to-wine story certainly doesn't swing the kind of clout wielded by the tale of Jesus' calling Lazarus from the tomb. It's not a blockbuster like the action-packed scene when Jesus ran the money-changers out of the temple. Or is it? Wait! A second look may explain why John dropped this drama in as one of his lead-off numbers. Actually, it is one of the richest moments in the Gospel. Not only does this story set the tone for Jesus' dealings with people, it embodies his principle attitude toward human beings: He starts where they are! And he always seems more concerned about the direction people are headed than the speed they are traveling or the distance they have come.

But before we jump into the story, it might be wise to clarify a couple of things that it doesn't tell us. First, the water-to-wine incident was *not* intended to cast a vote for booze. Some people fasten on to this text to support a little "tip of the bottle" now and then. That is not what the story is about. And to reduce it to that level is to miss the point entirely!

Some overspiritualize the passage, saying, "The water of the law is replaced by the wine of the Spirit" or "Not the water of ritual, but the wine of a relationship" or "Once the water of legalism, now the wine of grace." Good ideas! But not the point of Jesus' wedding miracle.

> JESUS WAS OBVIOUSLY VERY MUCH *AVAILABLE* TO PEOPLE.

Actually, Jesus gives us here a very practical but powerful lesson on kindness. God responds to the most "human" of problems: social embarrassment. And he starts with people where they are!

Jesus Was *Available*—He Enjoyed Being with People

Don't miss something subtle but profound on the surface of this story: the simple fact that Jesus showed up at a wedding. This means Jesus was obviously very much *available* to people. He was involved in the normal processes of human living. Besides, weddings are celebrations, which tells us that Jesus was available at a place where people were celebrating. Deity descended and partied with people.

Some people seem to think that Christians are supposed to wear a sign that says, "No fun, no sun, and no laughs." They're the dreary crowd with solemn faces and sourpuss expressions who spend long nights at home. The "really spiritual" Christian knows how to turn down invitations, turn up his nose at jokes, and turn her back on anything that seems to suggest a good time.

Obviously, not so with Jesus. The very fact that he was even *invited* to the wedding suggests that people enjoyed being around him and that he enjoyed being with people. Apparently, he was likeable, approachable, huggable. And he knew how to listen. Doubtless, he knew how to throw back his head and flood a room with laughter. His Father's love made him *connect* with people, not *dodge* them. Jesus was a life-lover. In fact, he said in John 10:10, "I have come that they may have life, and have it to the full." Note these wise words of Charles Spurgeon:

An individual who has no geniality about him had better be an undertaker, and bury the dead, for he will never succeed in influencing the living…. I commend cheerfulness to all who would win souls; not levity and frothiness, but a genial happy spirit. There are more flies caught with honey than with vinegar, and there will be more souls led to heaven by a man who wears heaven in his face than by one who bears Tartarus in his looks.

Sing Christian, wherever you go; try, if you can, to wash your face every morning in a bath of praise. When you go down from your chamber, never to look on men till you have first looked on your God; and when you have looked on Him, seek to come down with a face beaming with joy. Carry a smile, for you will cheer up many a way-worn pilgrim by it.[1]

If anyone has reason to enjoy life, surely Christians do. Who else stands on such solid security or trusts in such promises or expects such a bright tomorrow? A Christian carries a key to eternity! If that doesn't make a person want to get out and rub elbows with neighbors at a picnic or join in the city parade or sing in the local choral group, then something is off-target. Oh, no! Social isolation is definitely not a Christian virtue.

Jesus and people. Always with people! This is the normal portrait of our Lord!

Jesus Was *Sensitive*—He Knew What Was Going On

This piece of Scripture does not specifically state that Jesus was *sensitive,* but again, that voice between the lines shouts it.

He Understood the Culture

Weddings back then and over there differed a bit from here-and-now nuptials. For one thing, those weddings customarily lasted several days. Guests and family gathered at sundown with the bride and groom for a long, candlelight procession to the couple's home. The entourage often wound through the soft evening twilight of the narrow city streets, singing and celebrating. In the gathering darkness, candlelight and joy glowed in the happy faces. After the ceremony, instead of a honeymoon trip, the bride and groom usually stayed at their home for several days, reigning like a king and queen.[2]

There was gift giving, speech making, food eating, and, you guessed it, lots of wine drinking. Gifts, food, and wine were matters of high protocol. The food was to be well prepared. The wine flowed in abundance. And if you showed up with an inappropriate gift, the bride and groom could bar you permanently from polite circles.

Worst of all, if you wanted to be thoroughly humiliated as a host, just run short on food or wine. Jesus knew this was not merely an embarrassing little bobble in the kitchen. Oh, no! It was a blunder of unthinkable magnitude—a total disgrace to the family. After all, folks had come from great distances to answer your invitation. And what with no McDonald's, no 7-11, no Visa or American Express, the guests were totally dependent on their host. These social customs were taken so seriously that guests could actually bring a lawsuit if they were not properly cared for. So when Mary took Jesus off to one side and whispered, "They have no more wine," it was no casual observation. She was sounding an alarm.

At first glance, it may appear that Jesus was reluctant to help. "Dear woman, why do you involve me? My time has not yet come," he responded (John 2:4).

Jesus followed a clear time line. His life was not lived out in a vague cloud of random happenings. He moved toward a purpose, working according to God's timetable.

However, in this situation, Jesus faced a conflict between the urgency of his "Kingdom-preaching" mission and the human needs of the hour. This surprise emergency disturbed a well-laid agenda and disrupted its comfortable progress.

He Knew When to Deviate from His Agenda

In our day of Palm Pilots, cell phones, e-mails, and time management, there isn't much room left for sudden shifts in plans. The sacredness of our airtight schedules often squeezes out space for spontaneous responses to the people who pop up in our paths. And many are prone to neglecting real people needs for the sake of their schedules. Examples?

- the one who cuts short the phone call from a discouraged friend because it might make him or her late for a meeting of the "Compassion Committee"

- the preacher who defers responding to the grief of the church member because it's Wednesday and "everyone knows that Wednesday is for sermon preparation"

- the father who is too busy providing for his family to take a day off to love his family

- the mom who doesn't have time to listen to her teenager's life-pivotal question because she's got to clean the house

You may be furrowing your brow in disagreement. "But what is wrong with a meeting on compassion?" or, "Shouldn't a minister study?" and, "Is there virtue in a sloppy house?" The answers are "nothing," "yes," and "no." But we must remember that these are means to ends and not the ends themselves.

There is nothing inherently holy in a "Compassion Committee," for example, especially if that meeting keeps us from compassionate care for real people in crisis. And a preacher who ignores a hurting flock will have little credibility—no matter how well-crafted his sermons. And parents who consistently neglect relationship with their children in order to clean houses and pay bills are only kidding themselves about "caring for their families."

Now, please don't miss the point. Of course we need disciplined schedules. Good things don't happen without good plans, and good plans don't get worked without disciplined schedules. But when plans push people aside, something is off-balance.

This imbalance hit a ridiculous extreme early one Sunday morning. Ed, a staff associate in our church, had downed his last swallow of coffee and was headed for work when he heard loud pounding on his front door. Mary, from two doors down, burst into the living room. Utter panic blanched her face and distorted her voice. Just minutes earlier, Frank, Mary's husband, had fallen, crashed through a glass windowpane, and cut himself horribly. He was spurt-bleeding and in apparent life-threatening trouble. Time was running out. Mary had to get Frank to the emergency room—now!

> WHEN PLANS PUSH PEOPLE ASIDE, SOMETHING IS OFF-BALANCE.

Mary's panic shot off the charts when she knocked on the door of the neighbors between her house and Ed's. The neighbors had politely expressed their empathy with Frank and Mary's situation and said they were sorry but they couldn't help. With solemn, spiritual expressions on their faces, they had explained, "We would really like to help you, but we are late to church." They had "never forsaken the house of worship. God comes first, you know." Surely Mary would "respect that and understand."

Well, Ed never got to church that morning. Instead, he spent the day extending the Jesus touch to Mary and Frank.

Yes, this story is incredible, but unfortunately, it is also true. (Of course, in all the stories I relate, I change some names to protect identity.) And, of course, Ed's religious neighbors' actions could not have been further from the heart of Jesus. Sensitivity to people means that our actions will be determined by the needs of people rather than the events on the calendar.

That's what happened at the wedding. Jesus was following a serious agenda, but on the way, he was sensitive to people and responsive to their needs. These people were his friends, and he felt their critical dilemma, so he shifted his plans. But this is not the only time Jesus did this. Jesus shifted his agenda when the woman with the chronic hemorrhage touched his side as he was on his way to the bedside of a dying girl and when, on his way from Judea to Galilee, he encountered a Samaritan woman at a well.

But at other times, Jesus clearly chose *not* to change his plans, even in the face of what seemed to be legitimate and urgent needs. Like the time Jesus got word that his friend Lazarus was dying. Instead of rushing to help, Jesus stayed "where he was for two more days" (John 11:6).

How did Jesus know when to detour to the emergency and when to stick to his calendar? Divine insight may have played a part, of course, but a couple of practical pointers pop up here, as well. The next time the plans on your calendar conflict with the needs of the hour, ask yourself two questions.

First, *Is this a true emergency?* Jesus was willing to change when the emergency was a true emergency. This wedding host had his back to the wall. Wine *had* to be provided soon, or disaster could befall the family.

However, many apparent "emergencies," in reality, turn out to be long-standing problems dressed in the red flags of panic. By sometimes interrupting his agenda, and at other times sticking to his schedule, Jesus may be prompting us to distinguish true crises from chronic conditions—possibly serious conditions, but not immediately critical.

Late one night a panic phone call awakened my friend Ron. "Ron, its Mac. You gotta come over right away. Barb is threatening to leave me."

My friend Ron is the kind of guy who is always willing to go out of his way to help. But this time, he was due to leave before dawn the next day on business and wouldn't be back till the following Wednesday.

"Mac, how long have you and Barb been having serious problems?"

"Actually, Ron, ever since we've been married. Over five years."

"Mac, it is highly unlikely that one midnight conversation is going to fix a problem that has been brewing for years. How'd it be if I meet with you and Barb next Thursday? Things will have cooled down, we'll have more time to talk, and I will have more of myself to give you then. Besides, my flight leaves early in the morning."

"But Ron, Thursday is five days off. Something might come up—"

"Just write it on your calendar. Don't schedule anything else. Sounds like nothing could be more important than your marriage."

"C'mon Ron. Who knows what we will be doing five days from now...."

Ron didn't go. This was not really an emergency. If he had gone, he would not have helped Mac and Barb. In fact, he would have reenforced Mac's chronic irresponsibility. Indeed, as it turned out, by Thursday, Mac had actually "forgotten" his problem. Ron did the right thing.

A second question to ask: *Is there anyone else who can and should meet this need?* In the case of the wedding wine, only Jesus could meet the need. Most needs, however, can be met by any number of people. A few, of course, may be tailor-made only for you. And some are designed only for me! Maybe you have had personal experiences with problems similar to the problems at hand, making *you* the right person for the job. Or maybe I am closer to a certain troubled person than is anyone else. At those times, when only you can meet a person's need, the Spirit may be leading you to flexibly shift plans or scrap your agenda.

Jesus Was *Helpful*— He Met a Practical Need

When the host ran out of wine, Jesus went into action. He *did* something about it. "Bring me the water jars," he instructed, and they brought six stone jars, each containing twenty or thirty gallons of water. Something big was about to happen! Something that could not be ignored. Boom! Jesus instantly made more than 120 gallons of wine. By most standards, that is a *lot* of booze!

Jesus was being *helpful.* His availability and sensitivity would have been useless had Jesus not been willing to meet a practical need. He didn't cop out by saying, "I was sent here to preach not to turn water into wine. Besides, if I make all this wine, I'll trigger arguments in Bible study groups from now till the end of time!" No, Jesus saw a person in a tight spot and knew that only he could help. So he did! Simple as that.

Not just *available* this time. Not merely *sensitive.* But oh so *helpful.* The host got off the hook, the bride got blessed, and the ruler of the feast got a reprieve—all by what Jesus did.

Let's watch that: available, sensitive, helpful—and *creative.*

Jesus Was *Creative*— A One-of-a-Kind Original

Yes, Jesus was ever so *creative,* that most beautiful principle of the four. Remember, Jesus never treated two people the same. No one-size-fits-all approach to human problems. No franchised procedures, indexed to cover all categories: method one, drunks; method two, businesspersons; method three, homemakers, etc. Jesus didn't see people as units to be run through some canned spiel or process. He saw each person as totally unique and magnificently valuable!

To categorize people is to squelch their personhood and to slam our Father's creative grace. Not Jesus. He was and is creative! Since God has created each person unique, from his or her fingerprints to hair follicles, he intends that each person be treated special. And when we today show healthy regard for the uniqueness of a human personality, we reflect God's awesome nature.

Jesus Knew to Begin with "Felt" Needs

So note that Jesus creatively *begins where we are.* He met this man at the point of felt need—without implying either approval or disapproval for the man's performance.

Now, what *is* a "felt" need? Let me contrast "felt" and "central" needs. The central human need is spiritual. People are separated from God, alienated because of sin, needing a relationship with him. Most of the chaos in human lives can be traced back to a frustration of this real, central need for God. The surface symptoms of the frustration of this central need are what many call "felt" needs. People *feel* lonely or *feel* they don't have enough money or *feel* they are married to the wrong person. They may feel that they are too fat, too skinny, too tall, too short or

> TO CATEGORIZE PEOPLE IS TO SQUELCH THEIR PERSONHOOD AND TO SLAM OUR FATHER'S CREATIVE GRACE.

that they work the wrong job or serve the wrong boss—whatever! The surface problem is the felt need, but it is often perceived to be the real problem.

As we reach out to people, we must be cautious, however. Although the real need is spiritual, we cannot effectively address it if we ignore their feelings and shove them directly into "God-talk."

That didn't work for Ned. Ned is a bashful barber who was convicted by his pastor's series on witnessing. He got a man in his chair, lathered him with shaving cream, brandished his razor, and nervously blurted, "Are you prepared to meet your God?" We may admire the zeal, but his timing was way off!

Jon, our oldest son, played Little League with a kid named Timmy. Timmy's mother was a health-food nut. (Carolyn keeps reminding me, "No, she was fascinated with nutrition.") Timmy's mother believed that most problems—from emotional upsets to lack of coordination to acne or whatever—could be traced to a potassium deficiency. Everybody knows where potassium comes from. Bananas, right? She had convinced her son that eating bananas could fix just about anything!

So one day at practice, my son Jon was fighting a three-game batting slump, muttering to himself, "Dad says I may be taking my eye off the ball." Timmy overheard and got right up in Jon's face and asked, "Have you tried bananas?" Jon threw a bewildered glance at Timmy and then further theorized, "Or maybe I'm just swinging too late."

Timmy gushed, "Bananas. Have you ever tried bananas with honey and peanut butter?"

Jon backed away, shaking his head, and whispered to me, "Dad, that guy Timmy is *bananas.*"

Now suppose Timmy's mother was right, that Jon's coordination was off because of potassium deficiency and he needed to eat more bananas. Though Jon's *felt* need was a batting slump, his *real* need may have been bananas. But Jon saw absolutely no connection between bananas and batting slumps. So Timmy made no sense to him.

Just so, as we attempt to help people see their real need, their need for God, we must begin with their felt needs. That's how Jesus touched people—creatively. He began by addressing the unique felt needs of each specific person, passing no judgments on that person's feelings.

Jesus Knew When to Confront and When to Help

Here at Cana, Jesus met a felt need in a uniquely creative way. He could have seized the opportunity for a scathing sermon on the evils of alcohol—and what an opportunity! Just look at the stage props— six stone jars and possibly a dozen drunks.

But Jesus didn't do that. It was not the people-sensitive thing to do. Wine was not the point here; people were. And Jesus placed people far above issues.

Jesus did not operate at this wedding like one visiting evangelist who preached a revival at a country church during my student-ministry days. After months of relationship building, a lady who didn't know God and didn't trust churches finally consented to attend our revival. As she stepped from her car in front of the church, she took one last drag on her cigarette before entering the building. To the shock of all who stood nearby, the visiting evangelist grabbed the cigarette from her mouth, threw it on the ground, and verbally ripped into her: "Smoking dishonors God and rots your lungs and yellows your fingertips!" She looked horrified, stormed back into her car, and roared off the lot. Needless to say, she has never darkened a church doorway since. That woman didn't need a diatribe on smoking; she needed Jesus.

Jesus treats people more like some college students treated a lady we'll call Rachel. They met Rachel while working in a summer intern program in Miami, Florida. The students found Rachel sobbing hysterically on a residential sidewalk. She worked for a funeral home and had just accidentally switched two urns of ashes and delivered them to the wrong families. The poor woman was in a panic. "What am I going to do? I've just watched Lois grieve *again* over Harry's ashes, but they were really Tom's. How can I go back and say, 'Whoops, you got Tom. This jar is Harry!'"

NOT EVERY
SINNER IS A REBEL,
NOT EVERY
STRUGGLER,
A HYPOCRITE.

The students, rather than laughing at her or shaming her for such carelessness, contrived an ingenuous plan for one to distract Lois while the other secretly switched the urns. In this way, they met Rachel's felt need. In retrospect, we may see the situation as funny, but it certainly didn't look that way to Rachel. Through that "need meeting," the students began a relationship with Rachel and later led her to Christ. So as things turned out, Rachel's *real* need was met because the students creatively began with her *felt* need.

That same summer, some of the students met Bill, an alcoholic. They found him collapsed on the street, in delirium tremens from alcohol withdrawal. One of the students, guessing the syndrome, rushed across to a convenience store and bought a beer for Bill. Together they poured it down him! Bill could have died without some alcohol. Ask any doctor. The students then checked him into a clinic to dry him out. But they didn't stop there. They loved Bill into Christ. Unusual and creative evangelistic approach! Right? Not meant as approval for beer drinking, of course. But Bill is now saved, and the last I heard, was still an active Christian. The students coined a slogan to summarize that summer mission: "Ashes to ashes and a beer for Bill." Not exactly a religious slogan, yet like Jesus, they began where Bill and Rachel were. They creatively meet felt needs. They sensed that this would have been the wrong time to moralize, "Keep your mind on your urns and your hands off beer." Obviously that may have been good advice, but very bad timing, evangelistically ineffective—and definitely not Jesus' style.

The moment the host at the wedding ran out of wine was not the time for moralizing either. It was a time for Jesus to creatively care and help, by beginning with the man's felt need, rather than rebuking him for his failure.

Someone may object, "But doesn't Jesus ever confront people who do bad things?" Yes, of course. But not when he's trying to raise the faith level of a seeker.

At other times, Jesus most definitely did confront people who were rebellious and hypocritical. In the Temple, he confronted a bunch of religious crooks: They dressed like priests but cared nothing about God or man. They were dishonoring God and ripping off people. Jesus tipped their tables and cracked a whip and said, "Get out of here!" That's what those people needed. But not every sinner is a rebel, not every struggler, a hypocrite.

At the wedding, in the midst of this man's crisis, was not the right place for a sermon on booze. Jesus chose instead to be creatively helpful.

Helpful creativity means beginning where people are; it means being sensitive to surface hurts and wounds, even though you know the real problem lies much deeper. And creativity means helping people as they *let* you help them, not forcing them to take medicine they don't even think necessary.

In an ordinary city, at an ordinary wedding, Jesus met an ordinary human need, but in an extraordinarily creative way. The people running that wedding in old Cana were in a state of panic that day. More good wine was their felt need, and they couldn't see anything else. So Jesus began there.

Jesus' Glory Was Revealed in His Kindness

John says this was "the first of his miraculous signs" and that it *"revealed his glory"* (John 2:11). What glory? Was the glory in the miracle? No. Jesus' glory is not primarily that he is a supernatural winemaker or even that he is a miracle worker who causes people to say, "Well, I guess I'd better believe in this guy; look what he can do." Jesus' glory was revealed in that he saw and felt the needs of real people. This sign pointed out his concern for *people* over his own agenda or their poor performance records. He met the felt need of the host in a creatively unique way, without moralizing or passing judgment on the validity of the need or on the man for getting himself into this predicament. Now that's glorious. God cares about people! And we can reflect his glory by doing the same.

In this act of compassion, the disciples of Jesus saw his "glory," and John says they "put their faith in him." They believed. All the power of God went to a wedding and helped a host off the hook. And that moved these disciples to a deeper level of faith.

Remember: In the Gospel of John, believing is a *verb.* It's something that you *do,* the direction your life flows, not merely something you state or some abstract concept you hold on to. The disciples believed. Their "faith action" would be shown as they went out and treated people with kindness like Jesus did. True, throughout the Gospel of John, it is evident that the disciples' faith needed a lot of refining and clarifying as they assimilated Jesus' people-skills into their lives; but gradually, the glory of God shone through them more and more.

People really do need God. But they may feel symptoms that, on the surface, have nothing to do with "spiritual need." So "God-talk" up front may make no sense to them.

Jesus saw a variety of felt needs. Specifically at the wedding, he saw that the host "felt a need" for more wine!

"Not a legitimate need. Nobody needs wine," you object. Jesus' miracle is neither pro nor con wine drinking. It's about people-helping. Jesus did not feel obligated to approve of the felt need before he responded to the person.

What about us?

People Don't Always Feel Their Need for God

Each person carries his or her own unique feelings of need. There are as many felt needs as there are people. However, while all people need God, we cannot assume that they all *feel* that need. Much less can we assume, as do many believers, that all people feel guilt and long for forgiveness. Actually, thousands of people who are deeply involved in sin feel no guilt at all. At least, they do not identify their feelings with guilt. For example, people may feel frustrated because they can't manage relationships, or they may feel depressed or stressed or powerless over chemicals or a negative self-image. But they don't associate these feelings with guilt.

Martha was such a person. She caught me at breaktime during a seminar. She had just heard me say, "Just as the red light on the dashboard warns us to add oil before we ruin our engine, so a guilty conscience is the red light that keeps us from spiritual disaster. Christians cannot persist in hidden sin without being miserable. And that's good news."

But Martha disagreed. She told me she taught Sunday school in her church and had been married to a minister for several years. Then two years ago, she became a thirty-three-year-old widow. Martha confessed that since her husband's death she had become sexually involved with a married man in her church, the husband of a close friend. She had always believed that her conscience would kill her if she ever did anything so far outside of her values, that guilt would eat her alive.

But she said, "In all honesty, I am enjoying this liaison, and I feel absolutely no guilt at all. *I must really be sold to Satan!*" Martha added that she was terrified, precisely because her conscience was *not* bothering her. However, I couldn't help noticing that her hands trembled excessively. She said it was the Valium.

"Why Valium?"

"Nerves," she explained. Insomnia. Headaches. Piling on pounds. Chronically upset stomach. Martha felt all these, but she felt no *guilt!* She was unhealthy and miserable, but she had never identified her feelings as guilt. She took Valium to address the felt needs, the symptoms. But she ignored the real source of her pain. In fact she said the only time she felt good was during the sexual liaisons! Ironically, Martha was actually attempting to medicate her pain with the very thing that was causing it.

But How Do We Start?

Felt need is the place to start. But people are very private and guarded about their feelings. So if we are to connect with their felt needs, how do we surface them? Actually, the best way is through an authentic relationship. And these are two-way streets. This means we may need to be vulnerable about our own felt needs! One way to do this is to share scriptures that have helped *you*. When an insight from the Word of God helps you with a certain struggle, just dog-ear that page—either mentally or physically. Later when you sense in a friend a struggle similar to yours, you can say, "Yeah, sometimes I feel like that too. But something I read in the Bible helps me."

> WHEN AN INSIGHT FROM THE WORD OF GOD HELPS YOU WITH A CERTAIN STRUGGLE, JUST DOG-EAR THAT PAGE—EITHER MENTALLY OR PHYSICALLY.

Sue did this for her friend Patty. Patty, a non-Christian bank teller, came to the end of the day with her ledger off balance. She didn't know what to do; she was afraid she would get fired. She blurted out to Sue, "I feel like a piece of dirt!" Sue ventured, "I felt like that all last week. And you know what? I ran into something in the Bible that is helping me with that. 'God knows our frame, that we're dust'" (see Ps. 103:14).

Patty was no theologian, but this verse made perfect sense to her. "You mean that God knows that bank tellers screw up?" Maybe that verse doesn't grab you right now, but on that day, it directly connected with Patty's feeling of need. Sometimes we all need to hear God say, "I know how you feel." Sue had revealed her own felt need and, in doing so, connected with Patty's. Sue also helped Patty glimpse her real need for God.

And Now in Summary

As we visited the wedding at Cana with Jesus, he taught us something important about human relationships: Since a lot of people do not understand the root and spiritual cause of their misery, Jesus teaches us to begin with the *felt* needs and very creatively move them gently toward their *real* needs.

He begins with our humanity. But of course, he doesn't stop there. His ultimate aim is our spiritual need, and we see Jesus pressing toward this ultimate aim in encounter after encounter. But with each encounter, Jesus steps into a brand-new drama. To some he gives grace. To others, healing. Still others, a roaring lecture.

As we continue to observe how Jesus treated people throughout the Gospel of John, we'll see over and over again that he was *available, sensitive, helpful,* and *creative.* In these first two chapters, I've pointed out these characteristics very specifically; in future chapters, we'll explore these characteristics in a more general sense and leave some of the specific applications to you, the reader.

As we track Jesus through John, we will learn that whether a distraught wedding host or a curious rabbi, like Nicodemas, each person is different and is treated creatively in his or her own zip-coded way.

What about you? Do you treat people according to their unique needs? Read on.

Creative Touch

Begin with *felt* needs, then gently move toward *real* needs.

Thought Questions

1. What is the difference between a felt need and a real need?

2. How do we begin with felt needs and accept people without implying approval of sin?

3. Which is more important: the direction people are headed, the speed they are traveling, or the distance they have come? Why?

Action Questions

1. When did you hurry past someone who needed you? Specifically whom? Why do you think that happened? What will you do differently next time?

2. Who is a potential "wedding host" in your life now? How can you "make some wine" today?

Chapter 3

INSIDERS AND outsiders

ABOUT TALKING TO WHO IS LISTENING

What's a nice rabbi like me doing looking for the Galilean at this time of night? My colleagues back at the Sanhedrin will never understand. They'll think I'm sneaking around in the dark trying to hide something. And part of me says they are right. What does this hick-town carpenter know anyway? He's no scholar. I'm the one who is supposed to have the answers!

But God knows my answers aren't working for me. Haven't been for a long time. Don't even fit my questions. Maybe he'll have better answers. The crowds swear by him. Say they've lost confidence in the old ways. That I can understand. I keep the traditions better than most. Even the experts think so—they appointed me to the Sanhedrin—but no one has actually gotten much help from my "spiritual counsel." I guess that's the real reason I'm on my way to the carpenter. If your religion isn't working for you, you can't go on recommending it to others. Mine isn't, and I can't. But if that is the case, why am I afraid someone will see me talking to the carpenter? What have I really got to lose? My reputation, for starters.

Maybe even my livelihood. What would a man do for a living after he's been laughed out of the Sanhedrin?

But I'd gladly throw my whole career to the winds for the peace I see in the faces of the carpenter's friends.

Well, here I am. If he's got half the power they say he has, I'd best slip up on his good side. Here goes!

"Rabbi, everybody knows you're a teacher from God. No ordinary human being could pull off such wonders all by himself...."

Now there was a man of the Pharisees named Nicodemus, a member of the Jewish ruling council. He came to Jesus at night and said, "Rabbi, we know you are a teacher who has come from God. For no one could perform the miraculous signs you are doing if God were not with him."

In reply Jesus declared, "I tell you the truth, no one can see the kingdom of God unless he is born again."

"How can a man be born when he is old?" Nicodemus asked. "Surely he cannot enter a second time into his mother's womb to be born!"

Jesus answered, "I tell you the truth, no one can enter the kingdom of God unless he is born of water and the Spirit. Flesh gives birth to flesh, but the Spirit gives birth to spirit. You should not be surprised at my saying, 'You must be born again.'..."

"How can this be?" Nicodemus asked.

"You are Israel's teacher," said Jesus, "and do you not understand these things? I tell you the truth, we speak of what we know, and we testify to what we have seen, but still you people do not accept our testimony. I have spoken to you of earthly things and you do not believe; how then will you believe if I speak of heavenly things?"

John 3:1–7, 9–12

INSIDERS AND outsiders

ABOUT TALKING TO WHO IS LISTENING

Jim raises hogs. One morning he dropped by the local feed store for a few bags of hog "groceries." Jim slipped the clerk his order then stepped aside to cool his heels while the bags were loaded onto his truck. Behind the counter he spotted a large wooden sign bearing a painted message for all customers.

Checks are only accepted with:

1. credit card

2. local bank account

3. driver's license

4. telephone number

As Jim waited, another customer stumbled through the door. By his uneven swagger and whiskey smell, it was easy to tell that the man had begun to celebrate too early in the day. The drunk staggered up to the counter, blinked a time or two, and slowly read the sign.

Then he turned to Jim with furrowed brow and slurred speech and complained, "They ask too much! A credit card makes sense.

51

Two local bank accounts, well that is understandable. And someone *may* even have three driver's licenses, but who do you know that has four telephones?"

Point? Just because a message has been delivered doesn't necessarily mean that it has been understood. A word spoken isn't always an idea communicated. It's not only at Jim's feed store that the clearest-sounding messages reach their destination foggy and misunderstood.

THE RESPONSIBILITY FOR CLEAR COMMUNICATION LIES NOT SO MUCH WITH THE LISTENER AS WITH THE SPEAKER.

In fact, perhaps one the greatest means of serving others is through creative and careful communication. Simply throwing words into the air and assuming that you will be understood is neither sensitive nor smart. And it is especially unfair for "church people" to assume that the average person on the street can understand our shopworn religious jargon. Many good and intelligent people would love to know our Master if only we could skip the stained-glass lingo and introduce Jesus in language that makes sense to them.

Where the Buck Stops

Those involved in Christian communication (which includes all Christians!) must admit where the buck stops: The responsibility for clear communication lies not so much with the listener as with the speaker. Of course, the listener has some responsibility. But if we send fuzzy messages, even the most perceptive of people may not clearly decode our signals. As the apostle Paul said, "If the trumpet does not sound a clear call, who will get ready for battle?" (1 Cor. 14:8).

Jesus went to incredible lengths to get his point across. He drew inexhaustibly on stories, parables, case studies, and current events. And he didn't tell the same story to every person or even every audience, nor did he spout a repertoire of rehearsed speeches!

When Jesus walked in our world, he wasn't just a spiritual presence. He wore clothes just like we do. His feet got dirty and hot and tired like ours do. He hungered. He didn't like flies walking on his food. He strolled our streets through the thick of the people scurrying about daily business.

In fact, one historian reported that during the time Jesus was on the earth, at least 240 towns dotted northern Galilee, averaging as many as fifteen thousand people each. Adding in the rural population with the larger towns, this historian guessed that nearly three million people lived in tiny northern Galilee. So wherever Jesus went, people surrounded him. He couldn't make it to the market without touching sick people and well people, rich and poor, young and old, people from all walks of life. Jesus was always in the midst of people. Yet each was precious and unique, and a careful reading of the Gospels reveals how Jesus creatively tailored his communication style—not merely to each *audience,* but to each individual *person* he encountered.

Insiders and Outsiders

This creative flexibility shows up in chapters 3 and 4 of John's gospel, where Jesus encountered two people from radically different backgrounds. Their two histories were poles apart, and their felt needs were exactly opposite. One was a religious and cultural "insider"; the other, a definite "outsider." Jesus actually told the same story to Nicodemus, a male Jewish insider, and to an unnamed female Samaritan outsider. But he told it in two totally different ways. This is the Jesus touch.

The communication principles Jesus modeled in these two settings still apply today. In both conversations, Jesus allowed his message and his approach to be determined by the lifestyle and location of the listener—not by his own personal comfort zone.

Jesus was *available* to Nicodemus. If Jesus had a telephone, the conversation with Nicodemus may have gone something like this:

"Yes, this is he. Tonight? It's 1:00 A.M. Well. All right. Come on over. The porch light is on." Available, even late at night.

"Hold on a minute, Lynn," you may object. "We can't be that accessible to every crank who buzzes us in the middle of the night. Doesn't it bother you when total strangers call you at all hours? Surely we can't always leave our lives open to interruptions."

Of course, I do not mean to imply a life without boundaries. Interruptions must have bothered Jesus, too, because he was a person— just like you and me. But for him, the issue was not whether he was bothered by an interruption. For him, the balancing question was never "Does this disturb my comfort?" Rather, he was concerned with the way his response affected the people involved.

"Yes," you may ask, "but, if I am to stay available yet still keep healthy boundaries, who *are* the people I need to consider?"

The people in your family, for one. If I answer every call that comes down the pike, I will eventually damage my family. So when the call comes, I must clarify my priorities: At this moment, which is job one: the problem of the person calling or the present needs of my family?

This can be tricky, of course, and calls for no little discernment. I can easily become so protective of my family that I shield them from the reality of human need and send my kids the nonverbal message, "Don't worry about the rest of the world. We've got ourselves. Our neighbor down the road is not our problem." Balance is the key.

A second person to consider when that midnight phone rings is the person on the other end of the line. If I drop what I'm doing, will my response help or hurt? Will it give him or her dignity? It may. Or it may train that person to be further dependent, demanding, and manipulative and thus damage his or her dignity.

For that reason, Jesus was also sensitive to the "place" of his listener and fit his message accordingly. Our Lord, knowing that some people are insiders and some are outsiders, addressed the two in different ways.

Watch how sensitive Jesus was to who Nicodemus was. Some think Nicodemus sneaked over to Jesus in the night because he didn't have the guts to go in the daytime, too proud to be seen getting help from that Galilean carpenter. Well, maybe. But I wonder if Nicodemus may have come at night simply because he was a member of the Supreme Court (the Sanhedrin), one of the busiest men in all of Israel, and just didn't have time to come in the middle of the day. Point is, either way he must have felt a sense of urgency to come looking for Jesus at all, much less at such a difficult hour.

We know that Nicodemus was an actively religious man. Involved. Moreover, he tried to keep and teach the law. But apparently, something wasn't working for him. Yet he seems so much a part of the system that he didn't know *how* to travel outside his ruts. Because it was the way Nicodemus got things done in his world, initially he tried to "schmooze" Jesus.

A salesman showed up at our door one day saying, "I've flown all the way from New York City to see you because you're one of the leaders of this community. And if I place an encyclopedia in your house, everybody in town will want one." Nicodemus seems to attempt a similar approach with Jesus. "You gotta have special connections with God. We're all impressed that your stuff is superhuman."

Jesus could have interrupted, "Hey, man, manipulators I don't respect. Get honest or get out." But Jesus was *sensitive* to what Nicodemus was saying between the lines. He seemed to understand that in Nicodemus's world, manipulation was standard procedure. And more importantly, Jesus also sensed that behind the man's surface salesmanship lay a huge, honest desperation. So Jesus ignored Nicodemus's style and listened to the man's heart: "I've come here looking for something—I guess, for spiritual help." And in so many words, Jesus told him, "I've got what you're looking for."

Straight Talk for the Insider

Again Jesus was available, sensitive, and helpful. But to connect with the unique soul of Nicodemus, Jesus' touch was also *creative.* And this time, his creativity was terribly direct: "You've got to be born again." Bam! Just like that! In so doing Jesus continued to tailor his message to Nicodemus's unique capacity to comprehend. How Jesus addressed people was shaped, not by what he had read that morning or heard last Sabbath, but by the situation and needs of the person in front of him. So he treated each one uniquely.

Jesus knew he could be starkly direct with Nicodemus, because

Nicodemus was an insider. He and Nicodemus spoke the same language—figuratively and literally. Both had deep religious connections. Both believed that if you are to have a good life, you must have a relationship with God. Both believed that the Scriptures were the Word of God. Religion. God. And the Bible. A lot of common ground.

So Jesus could say, in essence, to Nicodemus, the insider, "You're involved in the religious establishment. You're keeping its rules. But something's still missing, right, Nicodemus? What you need, my friend, cannot be passed along in your Hebrew pedigree or through your institutional position nor your education—not even through your circumcision. It's your heart, Nicodemus. The only hope for you is to have a change in your heart and your nature—a change as total and radical as if you were actually to be born again. What you need is a new birth—a spiritual birth.

THE QUESTION IS, ARE YOU READY TO GLORIFY GOD?

"No more trust in bloodline, education, or religiosity. The question is, Are you ready to glorify God? That means, Nicodemus, you've got to go through a shift of identity as radical as the one the rabbis require of Gentile converts."

In those days, if a male Gentile converted to Judaism, he must not only be circumcised but take on a whole new Jewish identity, often even changing his name. In fact, one rabbi said that once the transition took place, the identity would be so radically new that a man could marry the woman who was formerly his own mother! The rabbis called this being "born again." Although Nicodemus dodged the impact of Jesus' statement at first, he understood quite clearly the implications of the radical and shocking confrontation with Jesus. "You got that, Nicodemus?" That's straight, insider talk.

Because Jesus respected Nicodemus's sincerity, and since they shared so much in common, Jesus could go right to the point. He wasted no time building cultural bridges. He didn't need to clarify vocabulary. He bypassed surface niceties, crossing bridges that already existed, and immediately declared, "You've got to be born again."

By being direct, Jesus offered Nicodemus hope. Jesus' blunt words essentially said, "Nicodemus, the people who don't love the light I am bringing will hide in darkness so that the light won't show them for who they really are. But I sense that you are different, Nicodemus. So come clean. Open up your heart. That's what you need to do."

What a creative touch! Oh yes, Jesus creatively tailored his blunt message to Nicodemus's unique place as an honestly struggling insider.

THERE WERE SOME PEOPLE WHO POSED AS RELIGIOUS INSIDERS WHOM JESUS KNEW TO BE OUTRIGHT PHONIES.

Of course, Jesus did not assume that all insiders were as sincere as Nicodemus. Quite the contrary. In fact, there were some people who posed as religious insiders whom Jesus knew to be outright phonies. And he knew that some people profess religion merely to impress other religious people. Some of his sharpest rebukes were aimed at that kind of insider. "Woe to you, hypocrites," declared Jesus, over and over (see Matthew 23). But he doesn't talk that way to struggling seekers or to those who, although ignorant and weak, are honestly seeking God. Neither does he bluntly confront the person who does not share his presuppositions. Even for Jesus, that would not only be poor communication, but it would dehumanize the target of his teachings. Yet with insiders who knew the vocabulary and how to work the system—insiders who abused people in the name of God—Jesus didn't mince words.

By Way of Contrast

Jesus' encounter with Nicodemus stands in stark contrast to his treatment of the Samaritan woman in the very next chapter. The Samaritan woman was not a religious person. She was a walking question mark in search of God and confused by religion. She came from the wrong side of the tracks, while Nicodemus came from the socially elite. Nicodemus came to Jesus' turf. Jesus went to hers. He found her by a Samaritan well. And since she was a different person, Jesus creatively treated her differently.

With Nicodemus, Jesus presented man's response to God's gift: "No one can enter the kingdom of God unless he is born of water and the Spirit" (John 3:5). Not so with the Samaritan woman. How could she respond to the gift when she didn't even know what the gift was? So instead of telling her how to receive the gift, he stimulated her to wonder what it might be: "If you knew the gift of God and who it is that asks you for a drink, you would have asked him and he would have given you living water" (John 4:10).

Do you hear the contrasting tones of the two conversations? Nicodemus already professed God. He operated from definite religious presuppositions and within clear-cut institutionalized structure. The Samaritan woman, on the other hand, was confused; she wanted

God but had heard so many conflicting reports on where to find him and how to worship him. And she had deep doubts as to whether she could ever be acceptable to God. Besides, she didn't seem to trust organized religion.

So, to Nicodemus, Jesus gave a *way* to respond. To the woman, he gave a *reason* to respond. To Nicodemus, he gave a *plan.* To the woman, He gave *himself.* Because Jesus and the woman lived in two different worlds, Jesus carefully constructed a bridge over which he walked from his world to hers.

With Nicodemus, we hear the sharp edge of expectation: "Are you a teacher of Israel and you do not understand this?" With the woman, we hear an invitation to hope: "Whoever drinks the water I give him will never thirst" (John 4:14). (More on this in chapter 5.) Two people. Two entirely different ways of touching people.

Robot Evangelism

One would think this is a very logical principle. "Of course you don't talk to two people the same way." But in some churches, as well as in a lot of believer-seeker conversations, this principle gets grossly underapplied. Perhaps you, like me, have been guilty at times of laying a set "spiel" on everyone we talk to—a one-size-fits-all approach, regardless of the uniqueness of the person.

Like me, you may at times have loaded your spiritual pistol with a prepackaged clip of verses and an explosively pointed question or two. (Such as, "If you died right now, why should God let you into heaven?") Then we go hunting. From door to door, in and out of shopping malls, up and down the streets, every target gets the same ammo. Same questions. Same verses. Same treatment. And what is the result? More often than not, we end up offending people in the name of Jesus, rather than building bridges over which Jesus can walk. Then we discouraged soldiers trudge back to camp wondering who is really winning the battle.

I am not knocking scripture memorization. Not at all. And I certainly do not discourage witnessing. Of course not. But I am saying that each person is unique and should be treated as such. Against Satan, we go to war, armed to the teeth. To win people, we go fishing! Using a different net for each unique fish.

And to get from insider to outsider turf, we must build bridges of relationship. Each person is valuable and unique. Each deserves to be treated with respect, even with a touch of awe. After all, each person is a one-of-a-kind creation of God, and "God don't make no junk."

The Jesus Touch

Legend tells of a kind and virtuous medieval king who was deeply loved by his subjects. The humble king, fearing that his popularity would go to his head, arranged for a respected member of his court to say several times a day, "Remember, O king, you are just a mortal." At times we need just the opposite. Human beings need reminders that we are not "just mortals." We are created in the image of God with value and dignity.

When we touch others with the touch of Jesus, we remind people from all walks of life that they are created in the image of God, beings of dignity and value in the sight of heaven. This is, after all, the heart of the Jesus touch. And remember, the Jesus touch was not meant to be applied only by Jesus himself, but by all of his followers—you and me included.

Creative *Touch*

Discern whether you're talking to an "insider" or
"outsider," and tailor your style accordingly.

Thought Questions

1. Recall a conversation where you have seen an outsider treated
like an insider, or vice versa.

2. When have you found yourself on the wrong end of such a conversation? Tell about it.

3. Describe the best example you can think of when effective
Christian communication connected with an outsider.

Action Questions

1. How can insiders improve their witnessing and worshiping styles
to more effectively connect with outsiders?

2. How do I get started?

3. What would Jesus do?

Chapter 4

A TALE OF two cities

SPEAKING THE RIGHT LANGUAGE

We killed a lot of lazy afternoons swapping stories
with the speakers up at Mars Hill square. A lot of us were
philosopher wannabes and loved kicking abstract ideas
around. Of course we were always on the lookout for new
material. Those out-of-town speakers from exotic places
could be especially counted on for something novel and
interesting. So I'd be front and center, all ears for fresh
ideas.

Word on the street rumored today's first speaker to be
something of a maverick. But a disappointed buzz spread
across the crowd when the first man up was nothing but a
wizened little Jewish rabbi. However, since I had nothing
better to do, I found a perch along the stone colonnade
and cupped my ear to hear what the man had to say.

Right away I could tell this strange little fellow was
no run-of-the-mill rabbi. First off, this Jew spoke polished
Greek! Second, he didn't thunder like an ancient Hebrew
prophet. More surprising still, he complimented us for
being religious—even pointed to a number of the stone
gods that stand all over our city. Then his index finger
stopped at one statue inscribed with the words "To an

Unknown God," and he began unfolding his gripping picture of this mysterious deity. But still no mention of the Hebrew holy scrolls. Instead, to my surprise—and pleasure—he rattled off some of our own Greek poetry! He actually used the words of Epimenides and Aratus to explain his mystery god.

I tell you, my friend, from that point on, this guy had me eating out of his hand. I didn't even turn him off when he claimed that this unknown god had actually raised a man from the dead!

Paul then stood up in the meeting of the Areopagus and said: "Men of Athens! I see that in every way you are very religious. For as I walked around and looked carefully at your objects of worship, I even found an altar with this inscription: TO AN UNKNOWN GOD. *Now what you worship as something unknown I am going to proclaim to you.*

"The God who made the world and everything in it is the Lord of heaven and earth and does not live in temples built by hands. And he is not served by human hands, as if he needed anything, because he himself gives all men life and breath and everything else. From one man he made every nation of men, that they should inhabit the whole earth; and he determined the times set for them and the exact places where they should live. God did this so that men would seek him and perhaps reach out for him and find him, though he is not far from each of us. 'For in him we live and move and have our being.' As some of your own poets have said, 'We are his offspring.'"

Acts 17:22–28

A TALE OF two cities

SPEAKING THE RIGHT LANGUAGE

On a crowded Washington, D.C., elevator, I asked my friend (loudly, expecting to be overheard by all), "Have you heard that Dan Reeves is to be coaching the Dallas Cowboys?"

"Naw, yer kidding," he replied.

"Yep," I said, "Reeves had that heart attack, you know, so now the doctors have told him to stay away from pro football." The D.C. elevator crowd broke into hearty laughter.

Since the joke went over so well, I tried it again a few days later in another crowded elevator—in Dallas, Texas. Result? I got mostly silence and icy stares. Same joke. Different location. Totally different responses. One from insiders and the other from outsiders.

Jesus' principle of unique treatment for insiders applies not only to individuals, but to whole audiences of people as well. You can see this in the New Testament as the tactical procedures of Jesus, our "commander in chief," became standard maneuvers for his "field officers," Paul and Peter.

Contrast the approach of Peter, at Jerusalem, in Acts 2 with that of Paul, at Athens, in Acts 17. Both are urgent messages delivered by

God's chosen spokespersons. Both are intended to call people to God. Yet the two radically differing audiences call for contrasting styles of language and pace and an awareness of the *location* of both speaker and listener. The speaker must be in touch with his or her own "cultural geography" in relation to the cultural geography of the audience.

In Acts 2, Peter is talking to a crowd of Jewish insiders. They are not "born again," but they are religious. Peter calls them "brothers." He appeals to Old Testament authority and deals with "religious" concepts familiar to the thousands in his audience.

Paul, on the other hand, in Acts 17, faces a crowd of outsiders. Greeks. Pagans. They don't know the first thing about the Old Testament and certainly aren't likely to be impressed by biblical authority. In fact, they have no Judeo-Christian presuppositions at all. Even the word *God* conjures up a totally different picture. So where does Paul begin?

Paul stands in the public square surrounded by statues and temples that are dedicated to a whole crowd of Greek gods and goddesses. And he says, "By the looks of all these gods around here, I'd say that you people are pretty religious" (not a compliment, just an observation). "I have some more information about the one you call the 'unknown' God."

No use quoting the Bible to Athenians. It would mean nothing to them. Rather, Paul quoted the Greek poet Epimenides, from a poem titled "To the Cretan":

> They fashioned a tomb for thee, O holy and high one;
> The Cretans, always liars, evil beasts, idle bellies;
> But thou art not dead, thou livest and abidest forever,
> For in thee we live and move and have our being.

Epimenides did not mean "we have our being" in Jehovah God.

He was talking about his favorite idol. So by quoting this poem, Paul spoke the language of the Athenians—outsider language.

Both Peter and Paul were applying the same relational and communication style that Jesus used.

Now how does all this roll down our freeways and ride our elevators? Let's make some applications. If we are to treat people the way Jesus did, what does that mean today?

Language—That's Greek to Me

First, it obviously means that we won't use insider language with outsiders. Jesus spoke the language of the listener. As a reader of this book, likely you are a "religious insider." Your inner circle may be largely church people. So as Scripture says, "Be wise in the way you act toward outsiders; make the most of every opportunity. Let your conversation be always full of grace, seasoned with salt, so that you may *know how to answer everyone*" (Col. 4:5–6). In other words, "talk to people in their own language." Choose your words carefully to connect with people who don't share your frame of reference. Just as each *person* is unique and valuable, and his or her feelings matter to God, so also each *audience* deserves to be treated with dignity and sensitivity.

E. H. Hutton relates a little story about Albert Einstein. While serving as a professor at Princeton, Einstein occasionally dropped in on the lectures of his fellow professors, lectures often so loaded with technical jargon that even postdoctoral students struggled to follow. As Hutton tells it, Einstein often took it upon himself to "rise after the lecture and ask if he might put a question. He would then go to the blackboard and begin to explain in simple terms what the lecturer had been talking about. 'I wasn't quite sure I understood you correctly,' he would say with great gentleness, and then would make it clear what the lecturer had been unable to convey."

These Princeton professors weren't the last people to lose their audience in gobbledygook. Hang around church circles, even for a short time, and you'll hear religious people speak a language all their own—with their own codes, slang, buzz words, and terms of affection. An outsider who happens upon one of these holy huddles may get an earful as confusing and obscure to him or her as a Princeton physicist's lecture to a freshman.

He or she might hear some "weird" sounds like: "propitiation," "expiation," "salvation," "reconciliation"! What a vocabulary! "Premillennialism," "Pauline theology," "fundamentalism," "Ebenezer," and "ebon pinion." And the shoptalk doesn't stop there. Try to explain *these* phrases to your buddies at the bowling alley: "for the remission of sins," "born again," "filled with the Holy Spirit," "washed in the blood," "Kingdom of God." Some inside the circle might figure out the terminology, but those outside might as well be hearing Greek.

George, an insider, was riding in the car with Steve, an outsider. They passed a billboard that gaudily declared, "Jesus Saves." Sensing a window for witness, George asked Steve what he thought of the billboard.

"Oh, I think it is great!" Steve replied.

"What do you mean?" George pursued.

"Well, I save, too! So I think it's great that Jesus [pronounced Hey-zoos] didn't blow his money. Hispanic people tend to be thrifty, you know."

Jesus didn't throw around faded clichés or worn-out words. He didn't dump obscure phrases onto his listeners, leaving the translation up to them. No, his mind spun tirelessly, persistently searching for fresh, clear, interesting ways to connect with people on the far end of his conversations.

Pace—The Times They Are A-Changin'

Second, in Jesus' communication style, he moved at the *pace* of his listener. He would never have been direct with an outsider, like the Samaritan woman. Nor would he have moved an outsider along as quickly as he moved Nicodemus—with his direct, blunt, insider conversation style. Paul applied these principles when speaking to the outsider Athenians.

A traveling businesswoman told me that her best "witnessing technique" was to sit on an airplane or in a restaurant and simply open her Bible and begin reading. "If anyone in the vicinity happens to be spiritually hungry," she said, "he or she will think, *That person over there reading her Bible must be a Christian. Maybe she can help me.* Then he or she might ease over and ask me some religious questions."

Now, my friend's technique may open a spiritual conversation with an insider, someone with religious presuppositions. But if the person near our Bible reader happens to be an outsider, when the Bible falls open, he or she will likely head for the lavatory or dive behind a newspaper. My friend's approach is exactly the wrong way to connect with an outsider.

This past week I did again what I often do. The person sitting next to me on the aircraft said, "My name is Kim, and I'm a nurse. What do you do?" I answered, "My name is Lynn, and I'm a writer." Sometimes I'm a writer, and sometimes I'm a minister. When I feel up for a visit, I may tell the person sitting beside me that I am a writer. Which I am. This opens some wonderful conversations. If I am tired and don't want to talk to anybody, I may admit that I am a minister, which I am. And that is almost guaranteed to stop a conversation dead in its tracks. When Kim asked what I wrote, I answered, "Oh, books, articles, things like that." Just as the plane touched down, I handed Kim a copy of my book *The Shepherd's Song.* She thanked me, opened the book, and saw that it began in the Bible with the life of King David. You guessed it: end of conversation.

If we continue to move at a pace that doesn't connect with our listeners, we can expect more and more religious conversations to end that way. Fewer and fewer North Americans are reared in religious settings. For example, in Washington state (one of the current hot growth areas of the continent), 80 percent of the people are unchurched. Outsiders. So if I base an argument on, "the Bible says," that fact may mean nothing to them. A large percentage don't believe in the Bible. This may be even more true of the formerly churched. George Barna points out:

> Less than half of our adult population will say that religion is very important in their daily lives. For millions of Americans religion will simply refer to a series of Sunday morning rituals that a shrinking number of traditionalists play. Less than 40% of the population...even associate themselves with a Protestant denomination. Barely one out of three adults...include church attendance on their list of things to do on Sundays.
>
> The '80s were a decade in which millions of young adults gave church another chance. But relatively few found much that was of perceived value, and the majority have again turned their backs on the church, perhaps permanently."[1]

How would Jesus touch these people? How should I? We insiders too easily forget. Ask my friend Larry. We chatted in the parking lot after a men's outreach breakfast. He had prepared for weeks and spent thousands of dollars on advertising. The plan called for Christian businessmen to invite a table full of unchurched guests to a breakfast. I was to speak on "Going Deep in Shallow Times." The purpose of this breakfast was to interest the unchurched guests in attending a seminar I was leading in that part of Dallas.

The turnout had been OK. Interest seemed genuine. But Larry was frustrated. He had sat at a table next to two other insiders and four outsiders. The insiders talked about church politics the entire time and virtually ignored the outsiders. Larry overheard similar conversations at other tables. I've experienced this myself. At businesses or civic gatherings, insiders often come up to me and start a church conversation.

One time I was standing in a service station surrounded by outsiders when this "insider zealot" came thundering through the door, charged right up, grabbed me by the lapels, and launched loudly into some recent insider controversy. I could feel the outsiders distance themselves from me—some permanently.

Even at church, not all visitors are looking for a church home. A friend may drag them in. Jesus would be available to those people, but not pushy, probing, or stuffy. And if he were to engage them in conversation, he would move at a pace comfortable for the listener.

Location—Your Place or Mine?

Third, Jesus' conversation was often determined by the *location* of the listener. He met people on their own turf. For example: He didn't require the bride's father at Cana to "come visit my church." He seemed comfortable in a nighttime conversation with a troubled rabbi at the venue of the rabbi's choice. And he considered a Samaritan well an appropriate place to talk of temples and messiahship. In each case, he was physically available at *their* locations.

Those of us who are veteran insiders might not realize the courage it takes for some outsiders to walk into a church. The setting is so foreign to outsider culture! Church people "act funny"—some super-solemn, others unnervingly ecstatic. Insider people interact differently too. They sit in rows and stare at the back of each other's heads, and they call perfect strangers "brother" and "sister." Sometimes they sit in silence and eat cracker fragments and drink little shot glasses of wine or grape juice. Often their music belongs not to here and now, but to then and there. Strange! Not normal, from the perspective of an outsider.

Jim Dethmer described the outsider perspective this way:

In Baltimore, a heavily Jewish city, I befriended one of the town's leading rabbis. This 86-year-old man and I used to get together to study the Old Testament. To show my love for this Jewish friend, I went to synagogue with him on a High Holy Day of Rosh Hashanah.

Let me tell you. That synagogue did not set up their service for me. I drove into a strange part of town. I didn't park in the parking lot, in case I felt the need for a quick escape. I walked up into the building. Nobody said hello to me. It was obvious that I was culturally different. Then it hit me that everyone wore skullcaps. I wondered, *What should I do?* I saw a big box of skullcaps and put one on. Most of the men wore prayer shawls. What should I do? Though I didn't know whether it was right or wrong, I decided to put one on.

This is an all-day affair and I couldn't find my friend, so I walked in and sat down all by myself.

Here's the cantor up there chanting in Hebrew. I had no idea what was going on. They were singing music I couldn't possibly comprehend. They were dressed in ways that made me feel totally out of place. No one interpreted things to me. No one informed me what I ought or ought not to be doing. No one made an overture to me in any way whatsoever.

It was an incredibly Gentile-hostile environment.[2]

This is akin to what outsiders often feel when they first encounter traditional church services. This is a formidable challenge even if the outsider is highly motivated to break in. In fact, in order for outsiders to understand the insider message in some situations, they may need to overcome even bigger social barriers than do Gentiles joining a Jewish synagogue.

Our very religiosity distances us from the people who need God most. One poet threw down this clear warning:

> We built a temple, beautiful and tall.
> We built it stronger than the Berlin wall.
> We built an altar, bright, beneath the belfry, where we could pray,
> forgetting hate and poverty, where we could find a refuge from the
> heat of human anger in the violent street.
> We heard the gentle voice of one who told of Him
> who talked of peace in days of old.
> Calmed were our souls till it would almost seem
> that Calvary was rather like a dream.
> We built a church out in the suburbs
> far from where the noisy, frantic people are.
> There we, caught in our tranquilizing trance,
> could meditate in holy arrogance.
> We built a ghetto out of shining stone,
> walled in from man and thus from God. Alone!
> —Author unknown

So what do we do? Downplay Christian fellowship, Bible study, and prayer circles? Disband substantive worship services? No. Worship is the fundamental business of the church. And while their primary purpose is for believers (rather than to be "secular seminars"), we can and should design our services so that outsiders can understand them and feel welcome.

Think about it this way: How would you feel if you showed up at our house at dinnertime and we projected body language and demeanor that said, "What are you doing at our dinner table? How did you get in here? All right, you can stay, but really, we weren't planning on it. We had no notion that you'd show up!"

Yet, all too often, when outsider people attend church, the environment makes them feel as if they are unexpected and unwanted guests.

But think how differently you would feel if you show up and heard words and saw body language that said, "You are welcome at my house for dinner. This dinner was prepared just for you." Somehow I believe that Jesus would plan church services that would feel that way to outsiders. And if we want to communicate with groups of outsiders, we may want to create services or events especially designed to connect with them. This might make more sense than expecting them to understand and appreciate a church service that is designed solely for the nurture of insiders and the worship of God.

Actually, Jesus didn't sit in church and expect people to come to him; he went out among the people. He sat in their homes. He spoke on their mountainsides. He walked among their sick. He held their children.

Paul the Apostle also picked up on Jesus' style: "I have become all things to all men so that by all possible means I might save some" (1 Cor. 9:22). Paul explained that to the Jews, he became a Jew. To those outside the law, he became as one outside the law. At whatever cost to his own comfort zone, like Jesus, Paul was willing to meet people where they were.

Christlike flexibility. Christlike sensitivity. Christlike adaptability. Call it what you wish, the point is the same: Say "God" in a language people can understand. "Do church" in a way that makes sense!

Some of our largest efforts have gone to care for ourselves. Most of our best speakers rarely speak to outsiders. Most of our best thinkers aim their thought-power at insiders. Even Christian mass media is mostly insiders speaking to one another—not to the world. How much of this does it take to snuff out interest and desire from outsiders?

Fresh Winds

In spite of all I've said, fresh winds are blowing. On rare occasions at first, but now more and more, we hear of creative outreach strategies paralleling Jesus' creative approaches. A few interesting attempts: One congregation converted a barn into a church building, in hopes of presenting a friendlier atmosphere. An insider family offers an annual block party in their outsider neighborhood so they can make new friends. Some new Christian radio stations are finally geared to reaching the secular mind, avoiding religious jargon and phrases. Contemporary music, media, and drama find their way into more and more Bible-founded, God-honoring church services. Churches' calendars and programs and styles are shifting in countless congregations to fit "folks who aren't there yet"!

When we see people through Jesus' eyes and listen to them through his ears, we will stand in wonder at the awesome variety of backgrounds and life stories swirling all around us. And we will go to any lengths—short of distorting the gospel, of course, to speak the *language* of the person God has put in our path, at a *pace* comfortable for him or her, and with a keen awareness of that person's *location*. Does he or she "live in Jerusalem" or live in "Athens"? When we catch Jesus' heart for people, our creative energies will be released—not merely to *announce* but to genuinely *communicate*. The Jesus touch knows what "city it is in," and "speaks Greek in Athens."

Creative *Touch*

Be aware of the language, pace, and location of the person God has put in your path, and creatively adapt your communication style to his or her needs.

Thought Questions

1. Tell about a time when you witnessed a communication exchange where someone was "speaking Hebrew in Athens."

2. Tell about a time you may have acted like a Jew in Athens.

Action Questions

1. What situation are you now facing where you feel like a Jew in Athens?

2. What steps might your church take to "speak Greek to Athenians"?

3. What can you do to reach across a cultural barrier—this week?

Chapter 5

THE ABANDONED water jar
STIRRING SLUMBERING HOPE

I first saw him sitting on the curb of the well in the heat. How strange. A solitary Jew in mid-Samaria? But I tried to ignore him and go about my work.

When he spoke to me, I froze for a second.

A man talking to a woman? A Jewish man talking to a Samaritan woman? Centuries of bitterness loom between our races. Some Jewish men don't even speak to their daughters in public, I've heard.

Is he making a pass?

"How come?" I demanded and spit the word *Jew* at him.

His reply was gentle and courteous, yet sounded like a riddle. "If you knew who I am, you would have asked me and I would have given you water—living water."

Well, I knew there was no running water here. Not any more. Thinking back now, my next question was insane: "Are you greater than our father, Jacob?" (I didn't know I was talking to God!)

My heart stopped when he suddenly switched subjects: "Go get your husband."

Why did he say that? My throat closed, and I could tell by the way he said it that he knew all about me.

"I don't have one." (It was a lie but not a lie.)

"You have had five."

Old hurts rushed back into my heart.

I asked him the question that had smoldered for a lifetime in my soul. I longed to know how to find God. Maybe he would know.

"On our mountain or in Jerusalem?"

He said it didn't matter. Said God was inside of us. Scary to someone as messed up as I. Couldn't I just figure out what was right and forget the inside? Sensing my search, he stopped talking about me and started talking about God.

I dropped my water pot and left it there beside the well.

When a Samaritan woman came to draw water, Jesus said to her, "Will you give me a drink?" (His disciples had gone into the town to buy food.)

The Samaritan woman said to him, "You are a Jew and I am a Samaritan woman. How can you ask me for a drink?" (For Jews do not associate with Samaritans.)

Jesus answered her, "If you knew the gift of God and who it is that asks you for a drink, you would have asked him and he would have given you living water."…

The woman said to him, "Sir, give me this water so that I won't get thirsty and have to keep coming here to draw water."

He told her, "Go, call your husband and come back."

"I have no husband," she replied.

Jesus said to her, "You are right when you say you have no husband. The fact is, you have had five husbands, and the man you now have is not your husband. What you have just said is quite true."

John 4:7–10, 15–18

Chapter

THE ABANDONED water jar

STIRRING SLUMBERING HOPE

Back while Carolyn and I were church planting in British Columbia, some of our financial support came from the mid-Southern states. We often went south for reporting trips. One Indiana Sunday afternoon, I described an unusual British Columbia wedding I had recently performed. The "wedding chapel" was an old cabin on the side of a mountain in the sagebrush just beyond the timberline. The bride was twenty-seven years old, and the groom was forty-seven. They already had two children, and the bride was seven months pregnant. But they were getting married because, as brand-new Christians, they had come to believe that the Lord wanted them to quit living "common law." Of the handful of wedding guests, five or six were alcoholics, some were drug addicts, and one woman was a prostitute who had often sold herself for a case of beer. Another man was on parole—attempted murder. All except two had recently come to Christ. There were no facades, no proud images to protect. At the end of the ceremony, instead of kissing the groom, the bride shouted, "Where's my rolling pin? I've got a license now!" Tears and hugging had filled the room. One of my favorite weddings.

But in Indiana when I described those mountain nuptials, one insider asked, "Don't you ever bring any good Canadian people to Christ?"

I've often wondered since, if Jesus had attended that mountain wedding, what he would have felt. I wonder, too, how this Indiana man would have felt if he'd been sitting on the edge of the Samaritan well with Jesus when the Samaritan woman showed up.

If there ever was a lady with a wounded soul, this "outsider" whom we first met in chapter 3 was one. She didn't hide it. She couldn't hide it. It was too obvious. Possibly her shoulders slumped from both the water jar and the weariness of her pain. Likely her eyes looked tired from ducking condemning glances fired in her direction. Her heart was scarred and calloused from the train of husbands who had said "I do" with their mouths only to say "I don't" with their lives. Her gait was difficult and slow as if each step were a trudge through the thick mud of her past. Perhaps half a dozen kids, each looking like a different daddy, tagged along stair-stepped behind her.

HE WAS AGAIN *AVAILABLE,* EVEN TO THIS DESPISED SAMARITAN WOMAN.

Maybe Jesus wondered what she was doing there at noon. Most people came in the cool of the morning. Perhaps she came for no other reason than a hot day demanded an extra draw of water. Or more likely, "decent" people didn't come to the well at noon. They cleared out so they wouldn't have to rub shoulders with the riffraff. Perhaps, for this woman, being shoved to this hour with the "trash" wasn't fun, but at least it cut down on the daily barrage of cheap comments and rude stares.

"Here she comes. They say she'll sleep with any man."

"Her kids are the worst on the street."

"Did you hear that she has a new lover?"

"The last one left her."

"What's love got to do with it?"

It was worth a walk in the hot sun to be away from the words that wounded so deeply.

Bridging Social Chasms

As surely as Jesus wondered what brought the woman to the well specifically at noon, she probably wondered what Jesus was doing there at all! One glance told her that he was a Jew. And in Samaria! "What was this Jew guy up to?"

Jews avoided Samaria at all costs. The shortest line from Galilee to Judea ran through Samaria, but most Jews would walk the long way around, adding extra miles on foot, to avoid contact with Samaritans. "Might get contaminated." "Hard to buy kosher foods."

But Jesus and his disciples deliberately walked smack into the middle of Samaria. He even stopped at a public watering hole—at noon—the hour of the riffraff, no less. He was again *available,* even to this despised Samaritan woman. That's the way Jesus was. The way he still is! His feet tread the turf of the people he's trying to touch. How can we connect with people if we step around the inconvenient times and unpleasant places where they live their lives? Jesus' heart for people wouldn't let him dodge the unwanted or steer clear of the unpopular. For him, each person was of immense value. So here again in Samaria, Jesus deliberately placed himself face to face with a person whom, apparently, no one else wanted.

Carl Sandberg told of frequent stands that Abraham Lincoln took against racial prejudice. One particularly stirring drama unfolded on the night of Lincoln's second inauguration ball. He had just delivered the blazing address in which he made famous the words, "With malice toward none; with charity for all; with firmness in the right, as God gives us to see the right, let us strive on to finish the work that we are in."

That evening, in a White House reception room, Lincoln stood shaking hands with a long line of well-wishers. Someone informed him that Frederick Douglass was at the door, but security wouldn't let him in because he was black.

Lincoln broke off from high-level protocol and had Douglass shown in at once. The crowd of guests hushed as the great leader appeared at the door. In a booming voice that filled the silence, Lincoln unashamedly announced, "Here comes my friend Douglass!" And then turning to Douglass, Lincoln said, "I am glad to see you. I saw you in the crowd today, listening to my address. There is no man in the country whose opinion I value more than yours. I want to know what you think of it."[1]

Those who see and respect the rich human qualities in individuals whom others reject blaze pioneer trails through thick jungles of bigotry. The next generation can walk on the path of such giants. What further delays might have impeded race relations in this country without Lincoln's heart and courage? This is Jesus' style as well.

As I write these words, I remember a long-ago wrong that still stings like a frozen lash. During our days in Kelowna, British Columbia, we came into an interesting circle of friends. Among them were Indians from a nearby reservation, as well as local civic leaders. The local Indian band occupied the low rungs of the social ladder and bore the brunt of racial prejudice. Ironically, I knew that several friends from both the Siwash reservation and the social register battled alcoholism. We'll call one Indian who befriended me "Joe Redfox." Joe was a street problem, notorious for wild bouts of public intoxication.

A friend from the other end of the social ladder, with whom I served a term or two in the leadership of the Kiwanis Club, was his honor, the mayor.

Now, in those young and tender days, I was quite self-impressed that I buddied with no less than Lord Mayor. I feel the stinging lash once again when I recall one particular Saturday: I was walking down the town's main drag when I spied my friend Joe Redfox coming toward me in the next block. Just as Joe raised his hand to greet me and I was about to raise mine in return, the familiar voice of my friend the mayor called out my name from the across the street. I halted my greeting before it reached shoulder height, dropped it quick as a flash, wheeled on my heel, and headed across to shake his honor's hand. I was glowing in the public attention I was getting from the mayor. At the same moment, I was pretending I didn't even know Joe, neglecting to return his warm personal greeting. My greed for prestige so overwhelmed me that I totally wrote off the dignity and significance of a very warm human being whom I called "friend." Though hopefully God has done some renovation on my character across the intervening years, my face still burns with shame at that memory. Why? I was so far from the heart of Jesus. So dehumanizing to my friend Joe.

God in the flesh was not only available to this woman; he was also *sensitive* to her. He read the signs that told the story of her troubled life. I don't know how Jesus picked up on all the distress signals. Maybe he'd already heard gossip, or maybe there was some subtle, indescribable something about her that spoke to him of sadness. Who knows? But somehow he realized that life had sent her little kindness. Perhaps John included this story in his Gospel because few could feel any more unwanted than this woman.

Jesus was sensitive, not only to the hopelessness of this woman, but also to the great chasm between them. He, a man. She, a woman. He, a Jew. She, a Samaritan. What do you suppose went through her mind as she walked past the man who sat on the well watching her— a Jew who actually opened his mouth to speak to her: "Could you give me a drink of water?" Was she startled, then shocked, then suspicious? Whatever she felt, Jesus most definitely had a hostile person on his hands! She was probably hostile toward men in general, but certainly toward this man, a Jew.

The Woman Nobody Wanted

Race lines in Belfast, Kosovo, and the Middle East could scarcely be more tautly drawn than those ancient lines between Jews and Samaritans.

It all began centuries earlier, when the Assyrians carried the northern tribes of Judah into captivity. The Jews had betrayed their heritage by intermarrying with the Assyrians, thus diluting their bloodline and creating a "mongrel race" called the Samaritans. Their religion became contaminated too. By the time the Samaritans returned to their homeland, their views of God were greatly garbled.

By contrast, when the southern Hebrew tribes were carried off into captivity, they stubbornly resisted the Babylonian culture. They returned from Babylon to Jerusalem, proud that they had compromised neither convictions nor culture. They would remind the Samaritans of the southern superiority at the drop of a skullcap. Even when the Samaritans offered to help rebuild the Jerusalem Temple, the southern Jews vehemently rejected their assistance, and more bricks were set into the wall of prejudice and resentment between Jews and Samaritans. So the Samaritans built their own temple; but in 129 B.C., a Jewish general destroyed it, a slap to Samaritan dignity that stung for centuries. Meanwhile, Jewish bigotry only deepened. So the woman who faced Jesus that day belonged to an *unwanted heritage.*

This woman also belonged to an *unwanted gender:* female. In the ancient Middle East, men did not reward femininity with special

> JESUS WAS SENSITIVE, NOT ONLY TO THE HOPELESSNESS OF THIS WOMAN, BUT ALSO TO THE GREAT CHASM BETWEEN THEM.

courtesies and chivalry. In fact, they systematically degraded woman. Some men wouldn't speak to women in public, not even their own wives or daughters. A few were so fanatical that they would literally close their eyes when passing a woman in the street. These were nicknamed the "bruised and bleeding rabbis" because they often collided with walls and trees while their eyes were closed. (Men today sometimes bump into things when they sight a woman coming down the street, but not because their eyes are closed!)

As if it wasn't enough that our water-bucket lady was from a throw-away culture and a throw-away sex, this Samaritan woman also seemed *unwanted by her own people.* Having gone through five husbands, she was now shacked up with a "lover." Her history of rootless romances draped over her like a sandwich sign, advertising to all that she was a social leper, not welcome at the morning well with proper people. She was a reject, shoved to the edge of humanity, a target of cruel jokes and lustful men. Doubtless, she could see nothing ahead but the empty drudgery of the water buckets and "wifely" bed of a man who wasn't even her husband. Yet way down inside of her, she had not stopped wishing that somewhere, sometime, some way, God would touch his people—that he would touch her!

For more than twenty-five years, Dr. Thomas Shipp was pastor of a great and caring congregation that began in his living room and grew to more than eight thousand members. Although in constant demand as a speaker, Dr. Shipp often went to small churches on preaching missions.

One Sunday evening he drove from Dallas to a small town to preach at 8:30. Some people standing around in front of the church said, "Preacher, see that house over there? (next-door to the parsonage, which was next-door to the church). A woman lives there with her seventeen-year-old daughter. A man drives up at ten o'clock every night. He leaves the next morning at two-thirty." They told Shipp that the girl was going to Kansas City and that everyone knew why she was going—she was "in trouble." Furthermore, they implied that the man who came each night was responsible. Shipp watched. Sure enough, at exactly ten o'clock, a man drove up and went inside. But he was gone in the morning.

Next day, almost everywhere Dr. Shipp went, people talked about this girl. Shipp asked the local pastor: "Have you ever been over to see the family that lives next-door?"

The pastor protested, "Man, I wouldn't be caught dead in that house!"

So Shipp decided he would go himself. He introduced himself at the door, "You don't know me; I'm Tom Shipp from Dallas, Texas. I'm over here preaching in the church. I understand that your daughter left town this morning. I just wanted to come by and let you know that I was thinking of you—this must be a difficult day for you. I don't even know your name, but I'm saying a prayer for you today."

The woman broke down in tears. When able to regain her composure, she explained, "I don't know what I am going to do without my daughter." Once inside the house, Tom discovered a third person, the eighty-five-year-old grandmother. The girl's father had died some years back. So the mother and daughter had come to this house to live with Grandma because Grandfather was also dead. Then Grandmother suffered an illness that demanded round-the-clock care lest she strangle to death. So the mother was completely confined to the house. No one in the community saw her. The daughter did all the shopping.

That evening, Tom arranged for a sitter for the grandmother so the mother could attend the revival. Tom introduced the woman to the congregation. "I want you to meet your neighbor and my new friend. This is a great night in her life. She lives next-door to the parsonage. Her daughter had to leave home this morning because they no longer had food to eat, and no one in this town would give the girl a job. Therefore, the daughter had to go to another town to work and send back money for her mother's and grandmother's living. Grandmother, who lives in the same house, is eighty-five years old and requires constant care. Your neighbor says she doesn't know what she would do, if it weren't for her brother who drives 120 miles every night and stays with Grandma between the hours of 10:00 P.M. and 2:30 A.M. while my friend gets four and a half hours of sleep. The reason this night is special to her is because it's the first time she has been back in this church since she was six years old, when her father was the *founding pastor of this church.*"

The woman by the church must have felt some of the same feelings as the woman whom Jesus watched trudge up the trail to Jacob's well. Because of social constraints, it was risky to help such people. No one would have blamed Jesus if he had pulled his robe over his face and ignored her. After all, he was tired. The disciples were gone, so who would have known? Besides, if he taught her anything, she probably wouldn't have the brains to grasp it or the spiritual framework to retain it. And even if she did, she had no credibility to influence other people with his message.

But our Master saw a person who mattered to God. As weary as he was, he quickly sensed a wounded soul badly in need of bandages, and he gently moved her into a nonthreatening conversation. But since he was talking to an outsider, he knew he would need to be unusually *creative.*

The Death of a Salesman

One interpretation of this Samaritan encounter floated in "sales-pressure evangelism" circles some time back. It went something like this:

Jesus asked for water. The woman became curious and was disarmed by Jesus' request. When Jesus saw that he had her interest, he manipulated the water bit around to *living* water. The woman grew more curious. Finally, curiosity made her vulnerable, and Jesus zapped her with a trick question about her husband. She ducked her eyes and tried to dodge the question with a half-true answer. "I have no husband."

Then Jesus sprang his trap, caught her in her dishonesty, and said, "You are right. You have had five husbands, and the one you're living with now isn't really your husband at all," as if to say, "Aha! Gotcha! You are not only a multiple-affair adulteress, you are also a liar!" At this point, realizing she had been trapped, the woman tried to wiggle out by changing the subject. She posed a theoretical religious question about which temple is the true temple. But it was too late. Jesus nailed her!

Now I ask you, does this sound like something Jesus would do?

I find it hard to believe that Jesus crossed his fingers behind his back while asking this woman for a cup of water! It's even more difficult to imagine Christ viewing her as a "spiritual trophy" and

> JESUS SAW A PERSON PRECIOUS TO GOD, A STOOPED AND BEATEN WOMAN WITH AN AUTHENTIC HEART, AND HE OFFERED HER A FRAGMENT OF *ACCEPTANCE.*

the water as bait. No, he saw a person precious to God, a stooped and beaten woman with an authentic heart, and he offered her a fragment of *acceptance.* By asking for a cup of water, Jesus was saying, "I don't feel the way others do. Your race, your religion, your gender, your past—these don't matter to me. You are a person. You mean something to me. In fact, *I* need *your* help! Could you give *me* a drink of water?" This account doesn't imply the emotional brutality that many suggest. Skip down to the result of Jesus' conversation. We find this stirring response: "Leaving her water jar, the woman went back to the town and said to the people, 'Come, see a man who told me everything I ever did. Could this be the Christ?'" (John 4:28–29).

Does she act like a woman who has just been caught lying about her sordid past? Just been snared in the trap of her own embarrassing failures? Why would someone who had just been humiliated by a total stranger run to praise that stranger to her family and neighbors?

And, be honest now, if the town tramp ran up to you and said, "Guess what? I just met a guy at the well who told me every bad secret I was hiding. Come meet him so he can do the same for you." Do you think you and the whole town would rush out to the well? Not likely! Right? But John says the whole town went out to see him.

What happened then? The key that unlocks this story is found beside the well: the abandoned water jar. And, somehow, I don't think she ever retrieved the thing. She had no more need to water the last dry sticks of a dead-end relationship. The abandoned jar speaks eloquently. It says that Jesus stirred a slumbering hope to its feet. It declares that this wounded woman found a joy so deep that she forgot to do what she came to do and took off to tell everyone the news, "The Messiah is here!" Instead of lugging heavy jars of tepid water to the house of a demanding human sponge, she piped in living water to all the hearts of a grateful, thirsty village.

What did the Samaritan woman learn? What had Jesus told her? We'll look at the "heart" of the matter in the next chapter.

Creative *Touch*

Imitate Jesus' courage to bridge social chasms and
his compassion to embrace the unwanted.

Thought Questions

1. Why do some people react with hostility when connection is what they really desire?

2. Why did Jesus' request for a cup of water from the Samaritan woman open her heart to his words?

3. What is the significance of the woman's abandoned water jar?

Action Questions

1. Who do you know who is separated from most of society by a chasm of prejudice or judgment? What can you do to bridge that chasm and offer the Jesus touch of love and acceptance?

2. Who is your "Samaritan woman" and how might you ask her for a "cup of water"?

Chapter 6

PLACES IN THE heart

LOOKING BENEATH LIFE'S SURFACE

When this strange Jewish man at the well asked about my husband, I froze. Then I stammered, "I...have no...husband."

Old hurts rushed back.

My first marriage began with high hopes. A beautiful wedding. Sometimes in my sleep I still dream that I am standing before the altar, wearing my bridal dress. Or that I am leading the candlelight procession through the streets and then dancing in swirls at the feast. Sometimes I dream of my husband and me and our children—all gathered around a table, with sunlight streaming in the window. But then I wake from my dreams to face cold, dark reality. That first marriage ended early and abruptly in heartbreak and humiliation.

My husband threw me out.

The second was worse. Lasted no longer. And ended the same way.

By the time number three came, I didn't really expect much. I felt like damaged goods, useless, hopeless.

"You do not even have the dignity and security of a husband, do you?" I heard the Jewish man say.

So when I spoke again, I felt that this Jew understood what was going on in my heart. He knew how I felt that day when I was turned away from home and children. Divorced. He knew how many dark nights I cried myself to sleep. He knew the real hunger at the center of my soul. And I had the feeling that he genuinely cared. He was the first man I ever met who didn't try to hurt me.

So I opened to him the question that for a lifetime had burned like an unquenchable flame in my heart: "Where do I go to find God?"

"God is a spirit," he gently explained. "Your heart is on a hunt for him, lady. You are on the right track. You will find him if you will be true and genuine."

Still confused, I said, "Well, I know the Messiah is coming!" You see, Samaritans, like Jews, expected a Messiah. "He'll explain all this to—"

His next words fell like lightning and shifted my whole universe. He looked me in the eye and explained softly, "You are looking at him this very moment!"

"Sir," the woman said, "I can see that you are a prophet. Our fathers worshiped on this mountain, but you Jews claim that the place where we must worship is in Jerusalem."

Jesus declared, "Believe me, woman,...a time is coming and has now come when the true worshipers will worship the Father in spirit and truth, for they are the kind of worshipers the Father seeks. God is spirit, and his worshipers must worship in spirit and in truth."

The woman said, "I know that Messiah" (called Christ) "is coming. When he comes, he will explain everything to us."

Then Jesus declared, "I who speak to you am he."

John 4:19–21, 23–26

Chapter

PLACES IN THE heart

LOOKING BENEATH LIFE'S SURFACE

My friend Clois often says, "There is always something going on behind what's going on!" He means that surface words or actions are usually merely symptoms of what is really going on beneath the surface of life. But Clois also notes that these surface symptoms usually appear to be totally unrelated to the real and larger issues in the depth of a heart. Thus, conversation focused on surface issues can leave the real issues untouched. But the Jesus touch gently moves from surface issues to the heart of the matter.

Both Jesus and the woman sensed that something was "going on behind what was going on" that day at the well. Jesus knew that the woman's search for water—and even for marital security—was only a surface clue to the profoundly deeper longings of her heart. The woman, on the other hand, feared that behind Jesus' friendly words lay either a come-on or some other sort of trap. So naturally, the woman, still suspicious, probed a bit more.

"How is it that you—a man and a Jew—ask me—a woman and a Samaritan—for a drink of water?"

One wonders what tone colored her voice when she reminded

Jesus that Jews have no dealings with Samaritans. Curiosity? Hostility? Did she spit the word *Jew* as if it were a four-letter expletive?

However, Jesus explained that there is a well of special water—the kind that can quench all thirst. See the wistful look in her eye as she pictures a life with no painful encounters at the well? "Sir, give me this water so that I won't get thirsty and have to keep coming here to draw water" (John 4:15). Can you hear her heart? This man not only accepted her but also seemed to respect her as she was. What is more, he offered her a way out of her past, a route that did not lead only to new burdens and some other bed! "Can this man set me free? Dare I believe he could, somehow, actually give me a new start?"

> JESUS EXPLAINED THAT THERE IS A WELL OF SPECIAL WATER— THE KIND THAT CAN QUENCH ALL THIRST.

But if this is what she imagined, the daydream of escaping her ball and chain of matrimonial failures seemed shattered as Jesus said, "Go, call your husband and come here." Why? What was Jesus doing? Was he trying to embarrass her into repentance? Hardly.

Jesus ached with the emptiness that had stalked the days of this woman's life. When she said, "I don't have a husband," she wasn't pretending that things were different than they were. On the contrary, in essence, she was saying, "He realizes that he has a humiliated person on his hands, someone whom life has not treated well. He also realizes that before him stands a person who has no hope at all."

"I don't even have a husband. I don't have *anything*."

At some special day in the past, she had celebrated her first wedding. Dreams radiant with joy. But before long came that other day, when her husband took her to the door and announced three times to the whole neighborhood (as was the divorce custom of that day), "I divorce you." Then she was on the street—alone, dreams shattered, destitute, facing prostitution or something worse.

Later, another romance came along and another marriage proposal. She went home with him, no doubt thinking maybe she had found a good man and a solid marriage this time. But a second husband also took her to the "divorcing door." How utterly devastating! But she had also felt a third failure, and then a fourth, and a fifth. Till finally, the ceremony seemed pointless.

When Jesus looked her in the eye and said, "I understand. You don't even have a husband," I do not believe it was a rebuke. Rather, Jesus responded, "You've had five heartbreaking experiences that have devastated you. Five of them! And now you don't have a husband. No security. No real relationship. No love and joy, no home that you can count on!"

So when the woman asked about the Temple, she was not dodging Jesus' point; she was plunging right into the middle of it. She was saying, "That's right. My life is so very empty. I desperately need God. Could you tell me where to find him?"

Moving from Symptom to Cause

Jesus had cut straight to the source of her pain. Authentic healing only comes when the true sickness is treated. Jesus teaches us here the importance of cutting deeper than the superficial and lancing the real source. He empathized with the hopelessness that plagued the days of this woman's life. He extended his hand to her, offering to enter the dark chamber of her world.

Jesus, do I see your thumb brushing the corner of your eye? "It must hurt, even after the pain of five desertions, the man you now live with won't even give you his name."

This Samaritan woman and this Galilean carpenter were not standing toe to toe in a hostile word game. No, they now stood heart to heart: Jesus the master surgeon and she the grateful patient. What Jesus saw here was not one more wicked whore (as some are prone to assume, but what Scripture does not say); he saw a brokenhearted woman who was still hungry for God. He saw a person who mattered deeply to him and to his father. And possibly, her first glimmer of hope was wakened, because she stood face to face with the first man she had ever met who didn't hurt her!

Before you tag someone "divorcée," you might pause to consider the sting that word carries. When someone loses a mate to death, he or she grieves and we pull alongside him or her and grieve too. His or her heart is broken, and something is gone that can never be replaced. But there is usually dignity in the grief.

But when a mate is lost through divorce, the same pain occurs. An unfillable void is created. However, there is no dignity in the loss and no real closure. So few comforters flow to the side of divorced people to help them grieve. Few stand with them in the loss and loneliness. In fact, the opposite often occurs. Some even look down on them through the scopes of judgmental rifles and fire subtle, piercing bullets of accusation. Someone who already feels like a failure in relationships is leveled to the ground by shots of intolerance and lack of forgiveness. This grief has no dignity. Besides, the "corpse" is still walking around.

Let's multiply that cycle by five and see if we can fathom the gaping wound in the center of this woman. She may not have been a bad woman at all. To me she looks more like the victim of five or six *bad men.* Perhaps she was plain. Maybe she came from a poor neighborhood. Maybe she couldn't carry on a conversation. Maybe she was missing her two front teeth. We don't know why she was so rejected. Whatever the reasons, layer by layer, the viciousness of these men had stripped her down until there was little left that was fine in her nature. Yet these vicious men had not stripped away her hunger for God, her hope for a coming Messiah!

A Hungry Heart

Ironically, those who have suffered the most often become the most spiritually insightful. Maybe it's because they have more reason to think on spiritual things. Or maybe because their very desperation sharpens the focus of their search for something that might take them out of their distress. Again, whatever the reasons, this woman's next comment reveals a long, tenacious pilgrimage in search of God!

"Our fathers worshiped on this mountain, but you Jews claim that the place where we must worship is Jerusalem" (John 4:20). In other words, "I really do want to know God, but I don't know where to find him! You people say he is in the Temple. My people say he is on the mountain. I have investigated both places, and I didn't find much 'God' going on in either one. You seem to know what you are talking about. Who do I believe?"

What did you feel as you read those words? You may have connected with this woman. Possibly, you, too, have long searched for God. Perhaps you, too, have found no answers for the questions that steal your sleep. Maybe, like her, you have heard the endless wrangling and futile arguing among the religious about religion and have walked away from a few visits to church feeling emptier than when you came. If so, the response of Jesus will be of special interest to you.

At this point, I picture Jesus becoming animated. He still gets excited today when he finds pure hunger for God in a broken human heart! I see him forget his weariness. Forget his hunger and the heat. I see him lift the jar off the shoulder of the woman and motion for her to sit down. And then he began revealing truths to her that up to that point, he had revealed to no one! That's right! The first person to whom Jesus revealed himself as the Messiah was a racially outcast, five-times-divorced, live-in girlfriend!

Let's paraphrase his response. "There is a day coming when the place of worship won't make any difference. You Samaritans worship what you do not know. You've been taught that going to the right mountain and performing the right ritual is how you find God. Ain't so. That is ritual; it isn't relationship."

One can imagine Jesus' finger punching the air as he continues unveiling the truth. "True. Salvation is from the Jews. But the day is coming..." He pauses and looks intently in the woman's eyes and discloses that the day has come when the "where" and "when" of worship will not matter. What really matters to God, he says, is genuineness in the worshiper. He cares most about what is happening in your heart.

Oh yes, Jesus saw her dark days. Felt her soul-hunger. "You are on the right track, lady. You're on the right track! Your heart is hungry for God, and you have never given up on your search."

Through Love's Eyes

Now, if you think eavesdropping on this dialogue has been fun up until this point, listen to the woman's next few words: "I know that

Messiah (called Christ) is coming. When he comes, he will explain everything to us" (John 4:25).

Look at that! Her question gives us a clue to the poor woman's heart. Remember, this is a Samaritan woman talking about the Messiah! Apparently this hope has kept her warm on all those cold nights. "In the back of my heart, for all these years, I've been dreaming of the day when God himself would come, hoping against hope that I could know him."

Can you imagine what comes next? Don't miss the drama. It takes my breath away. Don't miss the pure joy and the mist in Jesus' eye as he moves yet a bit closer and softly says, "The one you've been waiting for? He is here. *It's me.*"

That is why she trashed her water jar. That is why she nearly ran over the band of disciples coming up the trail. That is why she stopped the first person she saw in the village and said, "Come and see a man who knows every dream I've ever dreamt and every tear I've

JESUS SAW HER DARK DAYS. FELT HER SOUL-HUNGER.

ever wept. He saw my first wedding—white gown, flushed cheeks. He understood my romantic visions of a white house on a quiet street, of a baby babbling in the crib. He felt my delirious happiness.

"And he felt the deep, searing, relentless pain that I felt when I was taken to the door that first time and my husband called the neighbors around and said three times 'I divorce you.' This man by the well heard me crying on my lonely bed night after night. Rejection after rejection. He knew why I finally settled for a 'live-in.' He also knew those long nights when my heart cried out for God. He knew that I have hoped for him and longed for him. Could this man really be the Messiah? It seems too good to be true, but I think I just gave a cup of water to God! Now this man has come, and the chords that were broken will vibrate once more. For the first time in years, I feel hope!"

Then the whole village, thirsty for living water, came running out to meet Jesus. The living water does not flow to a holy house in Jerusalem or a holy hill in Samaria—and for this woman, not even to a happy home. If it had, she could never have drunk it. The living water Jesus offered flows to hungry hearts. The heart is the temple where God comes to live. It is the vessel in which we carry home the living water.

Jesus was looking for what was in this woman's heart. Love always sees the best; it always looks for the best. A little child of a Texas friend wanted to get a birthday present for his mother. He'd heard one of the older sisters say that his mother wanted a new slip. He wasn't real sure what a slip was, but he went shopping. When he stood in the ladies' department and was shown a slip, although he was mortified with embarrassment, he was still determined to buy one for his mother. The clerk asked, "What size does she wear?"

"Well, I don't know."

"What is she like?"

"Oh, my mother is just perfect."

So the clerk packaged up size thirty-four and sent it home. Next week his mother brought the thirty-four back and changed it for a size fifty-two! Love sees the best. And Jesus saw the best in this Samaritan lady: a *tender* heart nearly buried forever at the core of the woman's *tough* life.

Drop Your Sandwich and Open Your Eyes

Jesus' disciples came back from a grocery-shopping trip and found him standing by the well with a big grin on his face, staring at the disappearing figure of a woman who was hot-footing it toward town. The disciples didn't know what had happened. Jesus volunteered no explanation, and they lacked the courage to ask. One of them handed him a sandwich, and he turned it down. He was too excited to eat. Who could eat at a moment like this?

"Open your eyes," he told them. They looked up in time to see the excited woman disappear around the curve of the trail. "Look at the fields! They are ripe for harvest" (John 4:35).

Before long a crowd of Samaritans appeared around the same curve, with the same woman leading the pack. Smiling. Laughing as if someone had just told her a joke! The last time she came down that trail she was alone, carrying a heavy water pot and a heavier history of pain. This time, however, she came with friends. This time, she came unburdened and jubilant. "There he is!" she cried. They had come to invite this newly found Messiah and his friends to their town.

Talk about creative! Imagine the captivating scene. A handful of young Jews walk into town with a group of curious Samaritans. On any other day, if these two factions were found together, a fight would surely be brewing. But this time, they were drawn together by a common hunch, a common hope, that this unassuming carpenter might...just might...be the one they'd been looking for.

So the crowd headed back to town, following an odd couple: a Jewish man and a Samaritan woman, a rabbi and riffraff, incarnate God and a single mother, a long-sought Messiah and a long-rejected misfit!

As we follow this man-God on his brief earthly journey, we grow accustomed to his entourage; we frequently find him flanked by assorted castoffs. Tax collectors, harlots, crooks, thieves—they seemed to flow to him. Somehow they perceived that although he knew their darkest secrets, he was willing to forgive them. He felt their sharpest pain, too, and their deepest hunger, their longing for God! Somehow they detected that he could bring cleansing to their lives—so stained with forbidden fruit—and freshness into their stale worlds.

Calvin Miller, in *The Singer,* writes:

> "Listen, while I sing for you
> a song of love."
> He began a melody so vital
> to the dying men around him.
> She listened and knew for the
> first time that she was hearing
> all of love there ever was. Her eyes swam
> when he was finished.
> Then she sobbed and sobbed
> in shame, "Forgive me,
> Father Spirit, for I am sinful
> and undone…for singing weary
> years of all the wrong words…."
> The singer touched her shoulder
> and told her of the joy that lay
> ahead if she could learn the
> music he had sung.
> He left her in the street and
> walked away, and as he left,
> He heard her singing his new song.[1]

Such is the kind of joy that Jesus offered to the hungry-hearted woman at the well—and to us.

The Real Miracle

Much ado is made over the way Jesus healed physical illnesses. We also cover our mouths in awe at the way he mastered the storm or sent a dozen shrieking demons into the deep. Appropriate responses. But once we watch him treat the gaping wounds of this nameless woman, once we see the balm that he could so carefully place upon the lacerated souls, that's when we are left most amazed. This was where he performed his most majestic miracles and stilled his greatest storms: when he stitched together the ragged hearts of unwanted people.

Want proof? Look back at the well. The water jar is still abandoned. Want more proof? A whole town came out to meet the one who cared enough to notice "everything they had ever done" and to love them in spite of it. In fact, to love them out of it! To love me out of it. And you.

Creative *Touch*

Open your eyes to look beneath the surface chaos
into the hunger lingering at the depths of human hearts.

Thought Questions

1. Tell about a person in whom you saw "something going on behind what was going on." How did seeing this make you want to deal differently with this person?

2. What helps you see beyond someone's pain to the source of the sickness? How does true healing come?

Action Questions

1. Someone you know is hurting, but doesn't know why. What can you do or say to help him or her get beneath the surface to the real issue?

2. Put into words what is going on beneath the surface of your own life so that someone you love and trust can see into your heart.

3. Pray that God will help you remember what is going on in the heart of someone you find obnoxious because of the things he or she does or says on the surface. What steps can you take to minister to that person's real need? When will you do this?

Chapter 7

KICKING THE habit

LIFEGUARDING AT THE PITY POOL

Even from five feet above the pavement, the place smells bad. Garbage. Animal droppings. Stinking feet. Vomit. Used bandages. From my angle, it's far worse. I'm all crippled up you see. So my nose rarely gets more than belt-high. The smell gets to me. Been sitting in this old spot on this hard pallet every day for thirty-eight years. Mat gives me bedsores. Minutes inch by like years. But my only choice is to sit and beg—and take abuse from passersby.

And I'm so lonely. My pallet is too far from the foot traffic. But then, who would want to talk to a piece of dung like me anyway?

Life isn't fair. Why me?

What's that? Did I hear someone say that the carpenter is coming? I've heard he takes pity on people like me. Look. He's glancing my direction.

From close range, his eyes tell me he didn't come to hear me lament my predicament. Rather, he seems to be asking if I ever intend to rise above it. He offers no pity. But his touch feels like a lifeline thrown to fish me out of my pity pool.

Some time later, Jesus went up to Jerusalem for a feast of the Jews. Now there is in Jerusalem near the Sheep Gate a pool, which in Aramaic is called Bethesda and which is surrounded by five covered colonnades. Here a great number of disabled people used to lie—the blind, the lame, the paralyzed. One who was there had been an invalid for thirty-eight years. When Jesus saw him lying there and learned that he had been in this condition for a long time, he asked him, "Do you want to get well?"

"Sir," the invalid replied, "I have no one to help me into the pool when the water is stirred. While I am trying to get in, someone else goes down ahead of me."

Then Jesus said to him, "Get up! Pick up your mat and walk." At once the man was cured; he picked up his mat and walked.

John 5:1–9

KICKING THE habit

LIFEGUARDING AT THE PITY POOL

In the 1992 movie *Born on the Fourth of July,* Tom Cruise plays a Vietnam war veteran who is wounded, paralyzed from the waist down, and sent home. The young man who had been the picture of health, independence, and competitiveness merely sits around feeling sorry for himself and drinking. His self-pity drifts into rage. Then his rage shifts from bad to worse, until he alienates himself from his old sweetheart, his friends, and even from his own parents.

He hits the lowest point in his miserable life when he runs from relationships and reality and dives into a drunken tour of Mexican bordellos. But even a second-string prostitute spurns and ridicules him for his victim mentality. Once he has hit this all-time low, he finally begins to get hold of himself.

The movie has a happy ending, when Cruise forgets his self-pity and takes charge of his life. But few people who have fallen into the "victim mentality" ever leave their pity party and move on. In fact, all too many of us learn how to get mileage out of our misery, how to duck responsibility with our loser's limp and milk our misfortune for all it's worth.

Jane, for example, enjoyed her pity party. When Jane was the star of her high school track team, she sprained her ankle in practice. The doctor put her on crutches. The week prior to her injury, for the first time ever, Jane had lost badly in the one hundred meter race—to Bitsy, a longtime rival. Jane stayed on crutches for a whole week after the doctor said her ankle was ready for running. That kept her out of the next track meet, in which she was scheduled to run a rematch against Bitsy.

> DOUBTLESS, A LOT OF US ARE SUSCEPTIBLE TO THE ALLURING AND ADDICTING DRUG OF SELF-PITY.

In the meantime, Jane made a discovery: Without winning, or even competing, she was showered with more attention, especially from the boys, than she had ever received from athletic victories—until all the boys began to catch on and grow weary of her self-pity. Then Jane found herself surrounded only by less popular students who were attempting to raise their own social stock by "being tight" with the once-popular school celebrity.

Hooked

Doubtless, a lot of us are susceptible to the alluring and addicting drug of self-pity. It's the heroin of the emotions. It's the "angel dust" of the spirit. We may get turned on to it first during a period of adversity coupled with kind friends. The adversity may be sickness—perhaps cancer, a cold, or a broken leg. We may first take the drug to find comfort during a crisis: death, bankruptcy, or divorce. Whatever the cause, the treatment is often the same: Well-meaning friends treat us with pity. They hurt with us. They help us. They weep with us.

And most of the time, this treatment has its intended result.

Friends cheer us on. Healing occurs, and we pick ourselves up and continue with life.

Sometimes, however, the sudden flow of love and warmth and kindness feels so good that we keep coming back to the well. And gradually, with time, we become "pity junkies." Our helpers become enablers. We thrive on the compassion and attention of others. We yearn for someone to notice our plight or ask about our pain. At best our life is reduced to one objective: hunting for comfort and delegating our recovery to others; at worst, we cop out of responsibility and blame someone else for our problems.

Our conversations focus on ourselves: why we are sick, how much it hurts, how harsh the world is to us, why we are losers, and other assorted rationalizations for failure. We blame anyone, everyone, anything but ourselves. We become masters at reciting our woes. We hold out our tin cup to all who pass, begging for a listening ear.

"My boss doesn't respect me." "My children don't appreciate me." "Society expects too much of me." Or as my mother used to chide, "Nobody loves me, everybody hates me; I'm going to eat some worms!" Eventually, we end up miserable. We can't go on without our "attention fix," yet we don't like ourselves for needing it. We resent the very people we depend on to give it to us. And the bottom line of it all is anger—at circumstances, at others, and finally at ourselves. The quiet, bitter rage begins to poison every motive and every relationship. We feel unable to function, and we convince ourselves that we cannot. Perspective evaporates. Dreams are swallowed in smoke. Normal feelings of compassion and hope wither. And worst of all, self-respect lies charred among the smoldering embers.

The phrase *self-pity* embraces the word *pit* in its bosom. How cryptically symbolic! The pit is the end result of self-pity. A pit big enough for one person and no one else. The air is musty with selfishness, and the walls of narcissism block vision. Do you know someone addicted to self-pity? No doubt, you do. Then no doubt you know they are not easily helped. Partly because it's difficult, if not impossible, to help someone who wants to stay helpless. And partly because it's easy to get nauseated on his or her unending recital of personal mishaps and tragedies. And it is risky! You may wind up being the target of blame or overloaded with "leaners" or even sucked into a codependent relationship!

Would you like some insight on how to help people imprisoned by self-pity? To help this junkie kick it cold turkey? What do you suppose Jesus would say to people who live that way? Read again the story of Jesus healing the paralytic in John chapter 5. You will recognize, again, the four principles Jesus implemented when dealing with people:

- Be where people are—be *available.*

- Be *sensitive* to people.

- Be *helpful* to all people.

- Be *creative*—each person is unique and valuable. Each life a brand-new drama! No matter how unattractive a person has become, each one is valuable; each matters immensely to God!

Out Where the People Are

The man at the Pool of Bethesda is a classic case of self-pity. Thirty-eight years as an invalid. Plenty of time to become thoroughly convinced that he would never get better and that the world was enemy number one. Plenty of time to develop an addiction to the life of moaning, pity hunting, and blaming.

What a grim scene Jesus found at the pool. John said "a great number of disabled people used to lie" there (John 5:3). It must have been some sight. Bodies everywhere. Groans. Complaints. Stench. Begging. A scrap heap for broken-down people.

Some years back, I accompanied a friend as he traveled for treatment to M.D. Anderson Cancer Center in Houston, Texas. Most of my adult life, I have been no stranger to hospital visits. But I was not at all prepared for what I saw at this massive complex, known across the nation for excellence. Instead of the handful of patients with minor ailments conversing in a small waiting room, I saw large halls, filled with crowds of sufferers from across the country. All were strangers to each other. Most were desperately ill and living with the terror of a life-threatening disease. Most, far from home. As far as the eye could see: little children, chemotherapy patients with pale eyes looking blankly from hairless heads, elderly people who couldn't hold their heads erect, middle-aged skeletons pushing IV machinery ahead of their shuffle, loved ones with dark circles under terrified, tear-filled eyes. The clinical silence was disturbed only by the occasional groan or the racking sound of dry heaves.

As I sat waiting with my friend, I found myself thinking, *Surely this is the modern, high-tech equivalent of the smelly, suffering scenario under the covered colonnades surrounding the Pool of Bethesda.*

Again, the obvious may elude us: The simple fact that Jesus was at this pool is worth noting. He was where the hurting people were—he was *available*—even to a leaner. When we know that someone is a pity junkie, what do we normally do? If you know that a visit with so-and-so will end up with your being dumped on, do you want to go? Usually not. Life is already loaded with responsibilities, entanglements, negativism, and bad news. Who wants an earful of someone else's aches and pains? Who wants another draining dependent? Who wants to go to a person who chronically feels sorry for her- or himself?

Jesus does. That's who.

That is the way he is. The nature of Jesus is to go to those who hurt. Were he here physically today, he would be with the people in convalescent homes, hospitals, and mental asylums. Even with those who have a self-consumed victim mentality. If Jesus worked at your job, he would seek out the hurting people. But not just among the physically sick. He headed into all kinds of human misery. He wouldn't sidestep the inner city, with the winos, panhandlers, bag ladies, and cripples. And if my faith never leads me to these places and people, then maybe I should reexamine my faith.

George MacLeod underscores the availability of Jesus:

I'm recovering the claim that Jesus was not crucified in a cathedral between two candles, but on a cross between two thieves. On a town garbage heap at a crossroads so cosmopolitan that they had to write His title in Hebrew, Latin and Greek. The kind of place where cynics talked smut and thieves cursed and soldiers gambled.[1]

Asking Around

Not only was Jesus available to people in physical pain, but he also seemed especially *sensitive.* He saw beyond what ailed the thirty-eight-year-old crippled body to what ailed his *soul.* Jesus was not only willing to go to the mat with the man, but he creatively looked beyond the obvious to ask what brought him to the mat! "Jesus saw him lying there and learned that he had been in this condition for a long time" (John 5:6). He *learned.* Apparently, Jesus did a little asking around; he gathered some information.

A few mornings back a man stood not three feet from my car at the traffic light. His hand-lettered cardboard sign read, "I am homeless. My children need food. Willing to work." He eyed a ten-dollar bill lying on my dashboard. So I rolled down the window and, without saying a word, shoved the bill into his hand. The light changed, and I was gone. I'm pretty sure I gave him the ten mostly for my own benefit. I did feel better, but only briefly. Then I began wondering whether I had helped the man or dehumanized him. I certainly never acknowledged him as a person. I have no idea what he did with my ten dollars. He may have had no children and plenty of food. He may have spent my money on drugs. And he knew I didn't care enough to find out.

Later that day, I worked a few hours at an inner-city ministry of our church that distributes food and clothing. Here I interviewed another man who greatly resembled the man at the intersection. Following a form developed by the director of the center, I asked questions. Address? Social security number? Proof that he had applied for food stamps? I checked out his story. Reviewed his records. I asked about his family, his health.

NOT ONLY WAS JESUS AVAILABLE TO PEOPLE IN PHYSICAL PAIN, BUT HE ALSO SEEMED ESPECIALLY *SENSITIVE*.

Then I walked him through our employment resource and invited him to join our life-skills class where he could upgrade his employability. And although I never gave any of my own money and got no emotional buzz, and even though at some points my questions felt discourteously nosy, still I felt much better about my encounter with the second man.

I think it was more like Jesus to do a little asking around.

It is usually assumed that the man in John 5 was paralyzed. But the Bible doesn't specifically say that. Could his illness possibly have been psychosomatic? Had he just talked himself into paralysis? We don't know. But as we follow his story, we suspect it, and we're sure he had talked himself into helplessness.

Sure You Want this Medicine?

We get some clues about the man's helplessness from the way Jesus dealt with him! Jesus didn't avoid the down and out. But, then, he didn't encourage undue dependence on others either. Up front Jesus asked, "Do you want to get well?" What tone of voice flavored Jesus' question?

Did his voice sound like the compassionate shepherd? Trembling, on the verge of tears? Possibly. But I don't think so. Of course, Jesus felt compassion. And no doubt there were certain times when his voice quivered and his tears flowed. But not likely this time.

This time I hear our Master's voice sound firm, direct, and compelling. The Greeks could hear it clearly in the verb tenses. He was challenging the man to dump his denial, to get honest, to accept responsibility. He was telling the invalid to face up to himself. Jesus asked, "Do you *really* want to be healed?" Implying, "After all, you've got a pretty good thing going here. Your cup always gathers enough coins to buy your daily beans and bread. You have eaten three square meals a day for thirty-eight years. Everybody feels sorry for you. You have a lot of people looking out for you.

"If I were to actually heal you, Monday morning you'd have to be down at the unemployment office. At thirty-eight years of age with no job record, you'd have a hard time getting decent work. And if you did find employment, you could get fired or laid off or criticized or overworked. Are you really sure that you want to get healed? To face the facts? Or do you want to hold on to your story? Could your illusion be more comfortable than reality? I'm offering you an opportunity to become a person. Will you quit playing games and own up to your addiction?"

With these few crisp words, "Do you want to be healed?" Jesus probed that man's heart and left him wondering. Why else would Jesus ask the question? And why didn't the man react with something like, "What kind of question is that? Of course, I want to be healed. After thirty-eight years, what would *you* want?" But instead, the man's response was defensive. He complained! He rationalized!

Inadvertently, in his whining, the man further revealed his own spiritual paralysis. He told a tale he had likely told ten thousand times, "Thirty-eight years, and I've never made it to the pool. I'm a cripple, you see. Can't walk. Someone always gets to the pool before me. All these people stand around here, and no one helps *me*. It's their fault I'm not healed!" Meanwhile, we can't help but wonder if Jesus was thinking something like, *Thirty-eight years? Your body may be crippled, but your head isn't. Some days instead of begging for a shekel, you could have asked for a shove. At the rate of one awkward flop a month, after thirty-eight years, you would surely have rolled as far as the pool.*

Getting Clean

Jesus' challenge is intended for us all. Play with the drug of self-pity and you will dig your own pit. And with each spade of dirt that you throw out, you will be farther away from God.

If you are struggling with some painful "thorn in the flesh" that won't go away, here are some penetrating questions you may need to ask yourself:

- Do I really want to be healed or do I want to hang on to my "pitiful" story?

- Am I sliding toward addiction to self-pity?

- Is my initiative atrophied by my preoccupation with myself?

- Do I relish the attention others give me?

- Have I been abusing listeners with my whines and woes? Have I been trying to get by on my loser's limp?

Do yourself a favor. Throw away your needle. Flush your pills. You don't need any more "drugs." Get up off your self-made mat and walk. You *can* walk.

You have to take the first step. God is ready to cure you, but he won't help you as long as your medicine cabinet full of self-pity is more important to you than knowing him. Jesus also said, "Whoever would save his life will lose it, but whoever would lose his own life for me will find it!"(Matt. 16:25). The very name of the drug suggests its cure. "Self"-pity cannot exist if "self" is dead. We can't feel sorry for ourselves if there is no "self" to feel sorry for.

Conclusion

Yet we do not "lose our lives" by despising ourselves, bad-mouthing ourselves, neglecting ourselves, or punishing ourselves. These are still symptoms of self-focus.

If you sit by yourself for four hours on a hard bench, alone, in a cold, windy park, with nothing to eat or drink and nothing to read, soon all you can think about is how hungry and thirsty *I am,* and how cold *I am,* how uncomfortable this bench is *to me.* How slowly the hours pass *for me. How miserable I am.*

But add one ingredient to this scenario and everything feels different. Sit on that park bench with that fabulously beautiful person who is the one love of your life. The hours speed by with no thought of food, drink, hard benches, or chilly weather. What changed? The presence of a greater passion pulled you from your pitiful obsession with self.

We "lose our lives" by giving our hearts to something—to someone—bigger than ourselves. This shifts attention from self to another about whom we are more passionate than we are about ourselves. Jesus said, "If you lose your life *for my sake* you will find it." For Jesus' sake! He can bring us out of ourselves, to find life—full, giving, loving, and abundant life—in him. He may be tapping you on your shoulder at this moment, bending down to whisper, "Get up and leave this miserable pity party. Come on over to my banquet table and join the celebration of life!"

Creative *Touch*

Do a little "asking around" so you can distinguish
a legitimate need from a pity party. Then ask yourself:
"What is an appropriate response?"

Thought Questions

1. Tell about a time when you or someone you know didn't really want healing.

2. Is there any story you may be clinging to right now at the expense of reality? If so, what is it?

Action Questions

1. What steps can you take to break out if you are sliding toward your own "pity party"?

2. What specific, gentle steps can you take to help someone you know break out of his or her self-pity? When will you do this?

Chapter 8

DO YOU WANT TO get well?

FROM PATRONIZING TO PERSONIZING

Come to think of it, things could be worse. Sure, I sit on a hard pallet and beg every day, enduring abuse from passersby. But I'm secure. I have never gone to sleep hungry. An endless stream of do-gooders keeps dropping coins in my cup.

But I'm still not happy. No one ever gives me a break—not even a helping hand. Once every day the healing angel stirs the pool. First cripple in gets healed, they say. But never me. The able-bodied don't give me a tinker's hoot. So if you could just drop a few extra coins in my cup, old friend, God will be sure to smile on you. Thanks. Obviously you're one of the few who care about people like me.

What's that? The carpenter has come here? Yeah, they say he just lives for people like me. I'll bet he'll look me in the eye when I talk. He won't be stingy with his company, nor with his coins.

I think he's asking the gatekeeper about me!

Here he comes. Why is he looking at me like *that?*

"Are you sure you want to be healed?"

Do I want what? Is that any kind of question to ask a cripple?

The day on which this took place was a Sabbath, and so the Jews said to the man who had been healed, "It is the Sabbath; the law forbids you to carry your mat."

But he replied, "The man who made me well said to me, 'Pick up your mat and walk.'" So they asked him, "Who is this fellow who told you to pick it up and walk?" The man who was healed had no idea who it was, for Jesus had slipped away into the crowd that was there. Later Jesus found him at the temple and said to him, "See, you are well again. Stop sinning or something worse may happen to you." The man went away and told the Jews that it was Jesus who had made him well.

John 5:9–15

DO YOU WANT TO get well?

FROM PATRONIZING TO PERSONIZING

A popular school of thought among some mental health professionals of yesteryear explained human foibles by digging around in the past: How did your parents treat you? How were you potty trained? They implied that our parents and society are to blame for the way we turned out, that we are basically victims of heredity and environment. However, in 1965, psychiatrist William Glasser challenged that view in his book *Reality Therapy* and helped shift the shape of psychology over the last three decades. Glasser observed that, while factors in our past may be important, they are not determinative—that we do what we *choose* to do. And he insisted that people are *responsible* for what they do.

I first met Glasser while reading a description of his interview with a young woman who came to his clinic. She was on the run, in trouble with the law, abusing drugs, and surviving by prostitution (although she had come from an affluent family). The girl began unpacking her difficulties to Dr. Glasser by saying, in essence, "Well, Doc, my life is pretty messed up, but you know, I am emotionally disturbed."

Glasser would not allow the girl to hide behind psychobabble. His counseling technique was direct confrontation, and in words to this effect, he said: "How novel! We have shoplifters, prostitutes, chemical abusers, and runaways who come in here. But we don't have any 'emotionally disturbed' victims."

The girl grinned and replied, "Well, Dr. Glasser, I guess that's probably true, but I have gotten a lot of mileage out of this 'emotionally disturbed' [expletive deleted]."[1]

What would Jesus have said to her?

At least this girl admitted that she had become an expert in ducking responsibility for her own behavior choices.

However, this was not the case with a troubled college sophomore who came by to talk with me.

He longed to be a doctor but had little hope of it because his parents had not "done a good job of teaching him how to be responsible." So he didn't know how to study, thus he was flunking out of school.

Some time later, he came by again. Now, he'd married, but his wife had left him. He was still angry at his parents. They "hadn't taught him how to manage relationships." But he was also angry at his wife because "she couldn't help him be happy." Besides that, he was angry at the church because the church "didn't help him keep his marriage together."

But in a few more months, he called once more. He'd remarried, his second wife had left him, and he'd been fired. Not only was he angry at the parents, the wives, and the church—now he was angry at his boss because he was out of a job as well. And if I was any kind of "man of God I'd understand how life had victimized him and get him out of this mess!" What would Jesus have said to him?

Look at the next thing Jesus did with the man by the pool. Jesus was *creative* in the way that he reached into that man's life. He knew that people who are *paralyzed* easily become *patronized,* but Jesus wanted him *personized.* What does it mean to be paralyzed? On the surface, of course, it means that the person cannot physically move. However, physical paralysis is only the small issue here by the pool. The larger issue is that the man was psychologically paralyzed. He was crippled in his soul! Somehow, along the way, he had convinced himself that he was helpless—a victim!

But Jesus refused to patronize the man. "Get up!" he ordered. "Pick up your mat and walk." Jesus spoke in direct, demanding, confrontational language. Jesus personized the man. He challenged the man to take responsibility for himself. He demanded that the man go "cold turkey." He yanked the mirror out of the fellow's hands and forced him to look at the world again. And in doing so, Jesus was being creatively helpful, because whether the man was really physically sick or just emotionally sick, Jesus healed him. He said, "Get up! Pick up. Walk." Jesus' words were aimed at more than the withered legs on the bedroll. He aimed to straighten a crippled personality!

> JESUS REFUSED TO PATRONIZE THE MAN. "GET UP!" HE ORDERED. "PICK UP YOUR MAT AND WALK."

Jesus probed in the dark corners of a crippled heart to help the victim become proactive, to show him that there's a difference between *illusion* (the story that he'd been telling—"I'm a failure; I'm a victim") and *reality.* That even though he may have been ill, there were some ways he could take initiative for his own life.

This healing was not an easy thing to do. In fact, it would have been much easier for Jesus just to listen to the fellow's woes and whines, pat him on the head, whip up a few miraculous loaves and fishes, or dump some celestial silver in the man's palm and go back about his business—in essence, to patronize him. It is never easy to confront someone with his or her own addictions and illusions. But tough love doesn't always do the easiest thing. It is interested in doing what's right by a particular person.

The Confrontational Cure

What is more, Jesus called the victim mentality a *sin!* (John 5:14). When a person becomes so cocooned in a victim mentality that he or she is suffocating, then drastic action is required. One doesn't treat cancer with a Band-Aid. A flood can't be held back with tissue paper. And some "heart conditions" are so advanced that they call for "open-heart surgery."

Want some Bible examples?

Remember Simon the sorcerer? (Acts 8). He was the sweet-talking magician who actually wanted to buy the ability to give the gifts of the Holy Spirit. But when he made Peter a business proposition, the apostle showed how he earned the nickname "Rocky."

Peter answered: "May your money perish with you, because you thought you could buy the gift of God with money! You have no part or share in this ministry, because your heart is not right before God. Repent of this wickedness and pray to the Lord. Perhaps he will forgive you for having such a thought in your heart. For I see that you are full of bitterness and captive to sin" (Acts 8:20–23).

It wouldn't be too long, however, before Peter would walk the other side of the street. It seems that he compromised a bit himself. When there weren't any Jews around, Peter buddied with every Gentile in the church. Yet when the circumcised influential Jews, who were apparently his old cronies, came around, Peter gave the uncircumcised Gentiles a cold shoulder. He compromised the grace of God because he was intimidated by the law-conscious Jews.

The hypocrisy came to an abrupt stop, however, when Peter ran into a stick of dynamite called Paul. Paul knew that before things can get better, they sometimes have to get worse. He felt that brothers had a responsibility to bring out the best in each other, even if that is done at the painful expense of cutting off the worst. Paul's description of the scene is brief but sufficient: "I opposed him to his face, because he was clearly in the wrong" (Gal. 2:11).

Now, wait a minute, Paul. Isn't that overdoing it? What about patience and long-suffering? What ever happened to brotherly love? Of course there are many times when listening and sympathy are the perfect way to help someone. In fact, in a world so love-starved as ours, most of us could use a gentle stroke or two.

Cures That Don't Cure

But there are times when a compassionate ear only feeds a raging addiction. There are ways of "helping" that are not helpful at all. This is what it means to patronize people. There are times when love demands that we abandon the position of a listener and assume the task of confrontation. And there are times when doing what looks compassionate is actually cruel. Examples:

- delivering a Thanksgiving turkey gift or a Christmas fruit basket to a needy family across the tracks with no contact the rest of the year

- shoving money into the palm of a panhandler, rather than accompanying him on a shopping tour of the supermarket then visiting with him over a Big Mac or offering him yard work for pocket money

- dropping everything again and running to bail out Susie when she has let her car run out of gas for the twentieth time this month

- taking Johnny to McDonald's to console him after he lost his starting spot as wide receiver because he missed practice twice last week, all the while laying the blame on the coach for being unfair

We never help a person recover dignity and initiative by rewarding and reinforcing dependency and irresponsibility. Jesus didn't. We shouldn't.

When Carolyn and I were planting one new church, we had to get up early Sunday mornings, go down and sweep out the rented hall, and set up the chairs for services. Then we'd go and pick up people in our car. If we picked them up, they'd be in church. If we didn't, they didn't bother to come. We took it upon ourselves to make sure they got to church. But in doing so, we reinforced their dependency by taking responsibility for their behavior. We even learned later that some of these people actually hid from us to keep from being picked up! There is a difference between making people feel like a project and helping them to become a person—personizing them.

Sometimes parents are tempted to repeatedly bail their kids out of speeding tickets and bills and blame their coaches and teachers for everything that goes wrong. Consequently, some kids grow up to be emotional cripples. They don't know how to handle anything. Some try to stay in college (maintaining the minimum grade point average) as long as they can because "Daddy said as long as I'd stay in college, he'll pay the bills."

The same principle operates in marriage too. Sometimes one person takes responsibility for the happiness of the other. The other person says, "OK, you promised to make me happy. It's your fault if I'm not." Eventually, both are miserable, and it's the "other person's fault." We can't do for others the things they really need to do for themselves. We cannot "fix" people. If we try, usually their initiative declines, and they conclude: "I guess I'm not a whole person. I can't manage myself." They become less able to cope. Self-esteem shrivels and anger swells. Anger also builds in the person who's doing the helping when it becomes evident that he or she is being used.

COLLEGE STUDENTS WHO'VE JUST LEFT HOME EVENTUALLY HAVE TO REALIZE THAT NO ONE IS GOING TO TELL THEM TO DO THEIR HOMEWORK ANYMORE.

College students who've just left home eventually have to realize that no one is going to tell them to do their homework anymore. Nobody will tell them when to come in or when to get up. That's fun until the first test comes up, right? Who was it who said, "You can lead a horse to water, but you can't make him drink"? The same is true with us humans. You can send boys and girls to college, but you cannot make them think. That's something we all have to do for ourselves.

A college student, searching for self-discipline, once asked my friend Landon Saunders this question: "Landon, how do you get out of bed early in the morning?" Landon answered with a twinkle in his eye, "Well, the best I remember, when the alarm goes off, I put my feet over the side of the bed and stand up." Like Nike, Landon was saying, "Just do it!"

You can stay with the illusion that you are not capable of being responsible for your own life. Or you can accept reality and get up and on with it.

Of course, this principle holds as true with groups as it does with individual relationships. Some kinds of Christian charity, intended as acts of love and assistance, actually wind up damaging people and proliferating hurtful systems. As Roger Greenway and Timothy Monsma write:

> Churches and mission agencies that hand out food and clothing month after month and year after year are not really tackling poverty. Things need to be done that will break the poverty cycle for individuals, families, and neighborhoods, and lift people to a level where they can provide for themselves adequately and with dignity. Long-term relief only creates dependency relationships. As a consequence, large numbers of poor people have lost confidence in their ability ever to rise above poverty; they have resigned themselves to living off the benevolence of others.... There is a better way of conducting development ministry, but it requires a firm

commitment to using available resources in the most efficient manner, so that the poor are not merely fed and clothed today, but are empowered to meet their own needs, and the needs of their neighbors, tomorrow.[2]

Words of Warning

Jesus spoke some stern words of warning to the man at the pool: "Stop sinning or something worse may happen to you" (John 5:14). This statement raises at least two questions: How did the man sin? and What worse thing could possibly happen to him than already had?

Calling a Spade a Spade

First, what was the sin? After Jesus got the fellow on his feet, the man headed down the street carrying his mat, only to be stopped by a "church cop" who interrogated, "Why are you working on the Sabbath?" Rather than accepting responsibility for his own decision and his own behavior, the former cripple reverted to his old victim illusion. "Not my fault, man. It's his." And he fingered Jesus with the blame. "The man who made me well said to me, 'Pick up your mat and walk'" (v. 11).

So Jesus found him and said, "Stop sinning!"

"Don't do that anymore." Implying, I believe, "You are responsible for yourself. Don't slip back into your victim pattern." Jesus said, in essence, "You've been *sinning*. Sinning against *yourself*." The man had been sinning ever since he'd begun to play the "poor-helpless-me" game. Whenever a person sins against himself, he or she actually sins against God's design for him or her. Oh, yes! Self-pity and having a victim mentality is a sin. It is a sin because it focuses all of our attention inward. It elevates the self instead of the Savior. And those who would follow Jesus are told to "deny self" (Matt. 16:24). Not pamper self. Besides, self-pity often is dishonest because it avoids culpability.

God is calling us to something bigger and better than that. He calls us to take responsibility for ourselves and make deliberate, volitional choices and to live with the consequences of those choices.

That's why Jesus warned, "Don't sin anymore."

Result? In the closing scene of this drama, we see the man voluntarily go back to the Pharisee. But this time the man carrying his mat also carried his own responsibility. He admitted that Jesus had healed him (John 5:15). In essence, he said, "Not only did Jesus heal me, but I have made the decision to follow him. And I will accept total responsibility for the consequences of that decision."

> JUST AS SURELY AS
> PEOPLE CAN BE
> ADDICTED TO A VICTIM
> MENTALITY, THEY CAN
> ALSO BE ADDICTED TO
> "FIXING" PEOPLE.

Viktor Frankl said, "The last of human freedoms is the freedom to choose one's attitude regardless of the circumstances."[3]

The apostle Paul chimes in, "For God did not give us a spirit of timidity, but a spirit of power, of love and of self-discipline" (2 Tim. 1:7). When you accept responsibility for your life, God gives you the power to follow through! But he won't take responsibility *from* you or *for* you.

Something Worse Could Happen!

Now to Jesus' second warning for this man by the pool. When Jesus said, "Something worse may happen to you," what worse thing could that be?

Jesus wasn't threatening the man; he was explaining the facts of life. He was not saying, "Straighten up, or I will send you back to the pool even more grotesquely handicapped than you were before." Rather, Jesus was saying, "You will wind up doing irreparable, crippling damage to your soul if you continue on your path of blame and irresponsibility. You may end up shutting God completely out of your life!"

The life that is wrapped up in itself makes a pretty small package. There is barely enough room for one. There is certainly not enough space for someone as big as God. Those who choose to play the victim and deny responsibility do so at the expense of knowing God. That's a high price for a little attention.

If you've been blaming someone else for your failure and ungodliness and self-centeredness, or if you've used your pain to avoid responsibility, it's time to ask yourself this question: Do I want to live with the illusion that I'm a victim, or am I ready to accept the painful reality that I can choose to get out of, or rise above, this trap?

It doesn't matter if your spouse doesn't always care or if your boss doesn't like you or if your parents spanked you too much. Get up! God is greater than these things.

Addicted to Fixing

Just as surely as people can be addicted to a victim mentality, they can also be addicted to "fixing" people. These addicts are enablers of the "victim mentality" in another person—maybe even someone they love deeply. This addiction is kin to the Messiah complex. The feeling of power and significance that surges through us when people "cannot make it" without us. (Especially if they also give you a hundred and fifty dollars an hour to fix them.) Of course, legitimate counseling and therapy are valuable and helpful, but not the maudlin codependency that goes with some of the "shade-tree mechanic" kind of do-gooding we so easily get drawn into. This raises another set of questions that might clarify what we are up to:

- Am I a do-gooder who tries to make myself look nice without regard to how my "helpfulness" is enabling helplessness in others?

- Do I tend to cling to the illusion that I'm helping a person, which feeds my ego, when I may actually be hindering their growth toward responsibility?

- Am I willing to painfully, honestly acknowledge the realities in myself and gently, but just as painfully, confront the realities and hurt in the eyes of my codependent?

Dr. Sandra Wilson, in her book *Released From Shame,* helps us see very clearly that there is a huge difference between "sanctified codependency and authentic compassionate Christian service. The first [codependency] is motivated by self-protection, while the second [Christ-centered ministry] is motivated and energized by the Holy Spirit." In codependency, "people become statistics or projects to be 'won' or 'fixed'; but in authentic ministry, people are seen as being the same, all needing to be lovingly led to Jesus Christ as the Savior and 'fixer.'"

Dr. Wilson further points out that the enabler "enjoys serving most when the task is a monumentally big deal, but the authentic Christian servant will enjoy all service which Christ calls him or her to, even if the task appears small."

One who is codependent and manipulative "may demand external validation through public attention and appreciation, and likely will become resentful if they go unnoticed. The person, however, who is motivated by Christ can accept attention but doesn't demand it. He or she can remain unnoticed without growing resentful."

To the enabler, serving is his or her "source of identity and sense of worth in the church. But the person led by the Holy Spirit will experience service to God as an outgrowth of his or her identity as a loved, redeemed bearer of God's image."

In the name of "Christian love," the codependent may "bail others out, not expecting them to take personal responsibility for themselves. He or she may jump in and take care of others without waiting to be asked to do so. Those, however, who are motivated by the Holy Spirit will take responsibility for themselves under Christ's lordship and will let go of others to do the same."

As a "server," the enabler will "feel and want to appear competent and powerful, like a Savior. And the 'servee' will feel and appear incompetent and weak, like a victim. But for one who is involved in Christ-centered ministry, however, the 'server' and 'servee' have attitudes of mutual respect whereby neither feels nor appears incompetent, for they both realize their roles might be reversed at any time."[4]

We can paralyze people by patronizing them. Instead of paralyzing or patronizing people, Jesus personized them by seeing them as real people and helping them take responsibility for their own actions. You have likely already guessed that word "personize" is an Anderson original. But don't forget what it means. It means helping people become whole persons. That's what Jesus did. He deftly helped separate the victim's illusion from the reality of personhood and personal responsibility. And he did it because people mean so very much to him.

Creative Touch

Learn to "personize" people, rather than patronizing them,
by helping them to take responsibility for their own actions.

Thought Questions

1. What is the "victim mentality"? Describe a person you know who has the "victim mentality."

2. What are some signs to watch for when you think you or someone you love is slipping into a victim mentality?

Action Questions

1. What is the first step you can take to nudge someone you know out of a "victim mentality"? With whom and when will you do this?

2. What steps can you take to extricate yourself from a codependent or enabling relationship?

Chapter 9

DIFFERENT strokes

WHEN ONE SIZE WON'T FIT ALL

OK. So some people call me tight-fisted. But it doesn't take me long to reach the bottom line. And his idea was worse than impractical. It was impossible!

Before sunrise we had been mobbed with people. So we jumped in a boat, paddled across the lake, and climbed the hill just to get some peace and quiet. But it didn't work. The mob sniffed us out like bees would honey, and here they came again, swarming up the hill toward us.

The people had tracked him since dawn, so they were pooped. And starved. I guess food hadn't seemed important to them when they left home. But by now they had burned energy for hours and had eaten nothing.

Well, to put it mildly, we were all dumbfounded. The carpenter welcomed them as if all five thousand were expected dinner guests. Then, would you believe it, he turned and asked *me* to find them food. Had he lost his mind? There wasn't a bread crust within a day's travel. Besides, if there had been a supermarket next-door, who could afford to shop for that mob? One meal alone would eat up eight months of a fisherman's pay!

What he said made no sense! Yet something about the way he said it sent a shiver of anticipation up my spine.

Then Andy piped up, "This kid over here wants to share his sardine sandwich. It's not much, but it's a start."

Sure, Andy. Sure.

Andy has a good heart. But he can't count. Sometimes he is about as practical as three left feet.

Then the weirdest thing happened. The carpenter seated the crowd on the grass, said grace over the sardine sandwich, and started passing out pieces to the people. Only a kid's trail-snack. But the whole mob binged till they burped, and a dozen baskets full of scraps were left over.

He is the one who did it. The carpenter. Yet Andy, the kid, and I each felt that…well…that somehow, we had done it too!

When Jesus looked up and saw a great crowd coming toward him, he said to Philip, "Where shall we buy bread for these people to eat?" He asked this only to test him, for he already had in mind what he was going to do.

Philip answered him, "Eight months' wages would not buy enough bread for each one to have a bite!"

Another of his disciples, Andrew, Simon Peter's brother, spoke up, "Here is a boy with five small barley loaves and two small fish, but how far will they go among so many?"

Jesus said, "Have the people sit down." There was plenty of grass in that place, and the men sat down, about five thousand of them. Jesus then took the loaves, gave thanks, and distributed to those who were seated as much as they wanted. He did the same with the fish.

When they had all had enough to eat, he said to his disciples, "Gather the pieces that are left over. Let nothing be wasted."

So they gathered them and filled twelve baskets with the pieces of the five barley loaves left over by those who had eaten.

John 6:5–13

Chapter
9

DIFFERENT strokes

WHEN ONE SIZE WON'T FIT ALL

Bill Hybels cautiously refers to God as a "variety junkie." He doesn't mean this irreverently. Bill means that "God has a thing about *different-ness*.… I look around at creation and sometimes lovingly accuse God of creative overkill. Did you know there are three hundred thousand species of beetles? Now I ask you, wouldn't fifty thousand of them have been enough?… Isn't three hundred thousand sort of piling it on?"

But God also plastered variety all over the human race. "When each understands his or her unique circuitry, maybe we can celebrate it. Maybe someday even you will be able to fall to your knees and worship God for wiring you up exactly the way He did!"[1]

God graciously and creatively designed us to both give and need different kinds of strokes. He made no two people exactly alike. Just as our fingerprints are unique, each total human being is unique. Physically, emotionally, relationally, psychologically—we each play out the drama of life through our own unique plot. God loves it this way.

That is why Jesus encountered no two people in the same way. He creatively connected with the uniqueness of each new human being. No one-size-fits-all canned spiel. Jesus treated each person with respect and dignity, even with a certain amount of awe. He let each person be uniquely him- or herself.

If we do treat people with a one-size-fits-all approach, we not only show disrespect for the unique personhood of each human being, we actually show contempt for the gracious creativity of God! Think about it!

A Gang of Gifted Guys

Each person in the family of God has been given his or her own unique set of gifts and capabilities. Jesus understood this well, and he made it especially clear one day on a hillside above the lake.

Trying to get a break from the crowd, Jesus crossed the Sea of Galilee. But instead of peace and quiet, Jesus was greeted by a huge crowd that had followed him across the lake. When he climbed the hillside and sat down with his disciples, here came that huge crowd again, following him up the hill. So Jesus asked Philip, "Where shall we buy bread for these people?" Actually, Jesus already had a plan. Jesus saw a variety of gifts in his small band of disciples, and his plan would employ the unique giftedness of each one. Watch him creatively draw them out!

HE LET EACH PERSON BE UNIQUELY HIM- OR HERSELF.

Treasury Gifts

"Eight months' wages wouldn't buy enough bread to feed this crowd," Philip responded. Philip apparently had what might be called *treasury gifts*. He thought like a CPA, his mind quick with numbers: "Here's the average income. Here is the size of the crowd.

Here is the price of bread. Clickety, clickety, click! Conclusion: The numbers don't work. Eight months' wages wouldn't feed them."

Part of me is tempted to chide Philip, to accuse him of caring more about figures than about people, to remind him that balanced columns are not more important than full stomachs. But wherever Christians team up for a project, accountant gifts are needed. So before I knock the guy who always tracks the numbers to the bottom line, I must remember that God gave him that gift! God knew groups need balance between the accountants who tend to think in columns, and the visionaries, who, although they are indispensable, can sometimes be impractical. True, some bean counters don't see people. But on the other hand, some wannabe visionaries can do damage in the long run if they don't keep an eye on financial realities. No matter how bright and grand the vision, more people get blessed longer when the Philips keep good numbers.

Helping Gifts

Another person in that circle around Jesus offered a unique gift. Andrew, Simon Peter's brother, piped up, "Here's a boy with some bread and fish. Would that help?" Andrew had *helping gifts*. His heart cared. He was always searching for ways to help. He thought, *There's got to be some way we can solve this problem. This boy's sandwich and sardines at least make a start.* Sounds pretty impractical from an accountant's viewpoint. A can of sardines and a couple of biscuits to feed a convention center full of people! But Andrew didn't throw in the towel just because he couldn't yet see where all the money was coming from. Nor did it faze him that the boy might be left with no lunch for himself. His perspective was: In the face of such an urgent need, we've got to start somewhere!

Without the Andrews in our midst, the Philips would sometimes scare off all kinds of ministry. Without the Andrews, the Philips might choke on the numbers and kill the project!

Sharing Gifts

A third key person sat in Jesus' circle that day. He had *sharing gifts*. His name isn't even mentioned. He's merely "the boy with the fish and the bread."

Jesus creatively activated the treasury gifts. He anticipated the helping gifts. And now he draws out the boy with the sharing heart. The little fellow didn't have much, and he probably hadn't had much experience counting multitudes. Surely, he'd never administrated anything, at least nothing near this big. He'd likely never even fed a small group, let alone a mob!

That morning, the lad may have asked his mother for a lunch to take on his hike in the hills. But when he saw the hungry people, a heart like his couldn't help but share: "Here's my lunch. It's not much, but you're welcome to it."

Creative Collaboration

Then Jesus blessed the boy's biscuits and sardines. John the Apostle specifically explains that Jesus asked the people to sit down on the grass in companies, then he personally passed out the bread and fish. Everyone ate plenty, with lots left over. Even my wife Carolyn can't stretch groceries that far! Somehow, when God's fingers touch them, even the meager gifts offered out of our insufficiency can meet the needs of multitudes.

Again, we see that Jesus is available. And sensitive. And helpful. And again, he is incredibly creative.

But it didn't stop with that little band of helpers on the hillside long ago. He still "gifts" us when he calls us to work his plans. And he still uses a variety of gifts to accomplish his purposes today.

Gifts in the Bible

Beyond the Gospel of John, the rest of the Bible also has a good deal do say about "giftedness" among believers.

Three Characteristics of Biblical Gifts

First, clearly, *every believer receives at least one spiritual gift.* "Now to each one the manifestation of the Spirit is given for the common good.… All these are the work of one and the same Spirit, and he gives them to each one, just as he determines" (1 Cor. 12:7, 11).

Besides the spiritual gifts given to individual believers, the Lord also gifts the church with various leaders: "He…gave some to be apostles, some to be prophets, some to be evangelists, and some to be pastors and teachers, to prepare God's people for works of service" (Eph. 4:11–12).

Second, *Jesus gifts the church with a variety of leaders.* Paul exhorted Christians to use their gifts for "the good of others" (1 Cor. 10:24) "so that the body of Christ may be built up" (Eph. 4:12). And Peter said, "Each one should use whatever gift he has received to serve others" (1 Pet. 4:10).

Whatever unique capability God has given each of us is intended for the upbuilding of all. That's what gifts are for. They're not meant to build up a person's ego or prestige or following. Gifts are not given for personal celebration but to *build up the whole body.*

This is also why God gave the church the gift of certain leaders: so that "the body of Christ [might] be built up" (Eph. 4:12). These leaders are intended to nurture strong relationships, solid character, effective ministry, and rich Christlikeness.

Third, *we are not all gifted alike, but every gift is important.*

Peter and Paul Tell Us More

Paul explained to the church in Corinth:

Now to each one the manifestation of the Spirit is given for the common good. To one there is given through the Spirit the message of wisdom, to another the message of knowledge by means of the same Spirit, to another faith by the same Spirit, to another gifts of healing by that one Spirit, to another miraculous powers, to another prophecy, to another distinguishing between spirits, to another speaking in different kinds of tongues, and to still another the interpretation of tongues. All these are the work of one and the same Spirit, and he gives them to each one, just as he determines. (1 Cor. 12:7–11)

> WE ARE NOT ALL GIFTED ALIKE, BUT EVERY GIFT IS IMPORTANT.

Paul also reminded the church in Rome: "Just as each of us has one body with many members, and these members do not all have the same function, so in Christ we who are many form one body, and each member belongs to all the others" (Rom. 12:4–5).

Peter seems to lump all these gifts into two broad categories. The first category is the *speaking* or *teaching* gifts. Peter says, "If anyone speaks, he should do it as one speaking the very words of God" (1

Pet. 4:11). Peter's other category is *serving* gifts—"If anyone serves, he should do it with the strength God provides" (1 Pet. 4:11). What a balanced arsenal of spiritual weaponry: God's words for teaching gifts. God's strength for serving gifts.

Teaching gifts are no more "spiritual" than serving gifts, saying, "Truly spiritual Christians study the Bible and pray—like me!" A gifted teacher must not discount nonteaching gifts. Nor can Christians with serving gifts regard teachers less Christian because they "merely talk" instead of "getting their hands dirty doing service." God gave both kinds of gifts, and *both* are needed.

Paul gets much more explicit than Peter. Beside the list of nine gifts we just read in 1 Corinthians, Paul also describes seven gifts in Romans chapter 12: "If a man's gift is prophesying, let him use it in proportion to his faith. If it is serving, let him serve; if it is teaching, let him teach; if it is encouraging, let him encourage; if it is contributing to the needs of others, let him give generously; if it is leadership, let him govern diligently; if it is showing mercy, let him do it cheerfully" (vv. 6–8).

In both of Paul's lists of gifts—the long list in 1 Corinthians 12 and the short one in Romans 12—he makes it clear that we are not all wired the same way. Equally clear: While our gifts differ, one gift is no more important to the body than another.

Paul wants to make sure his readers understand that each person is valuable to God and has a role to play in the unfolding mission of Jesus. One may witness while another may be gifted with evangelistic teaching. Still another may have the gift of encouragement while someone else disciples others toward maturity. Still others serve with gifts of administration or giving or service or mercy. All gifts are needed. No one gift is more important than another.

CHAPTER 9

Prioritizing Your Ministry
around Your Gift

Of course my giftedness in one area does not absolve me from service outside of my gift. A servant-hearted person is willing to do whatever needs doing. At one period of time or another, each of us may be called to serve outside our unique area of giftedness. There is no task in the body I shouldn't be willing to try. Every player on the baseball team has to hit the ball. But not everybody is Mark McGwire. (I'm dating myself here.) So McGwire is a designated hitter. Every player occasionally has to throw the ball. But not everyone is Roger "The Rocket" Clemens. That's why he's on the mound. Each player wears a glove because sooner or later he will have to catch the ball. But not everybody plays behind home plate. So while every player occasionally hits, catches, and throws the ball, the coach must organize team positions around each player's unique gift. Just so, the Christian enterprise. Although everyone is called to be servant-hearted, each person is most effective and most fulfilled when prioritizing his or her major ministry role around his or her unique spiritual gift.

If "the ball is hit to me," I need to give it my best. I want to meet needs that fall in my path—whether I'm particularly gifted to meet them or not. But when I back off to prioritize my energies, to plan my calendar, to identify my calling, I must design my major commitment to fit my gift. If not, I may allow myself to be railroaded into tasks that make me nonproductive—and miserable! And I may find myself with no time to "play the position" God designated me to play "on his team."

Don't Cop-Out

A word of caution here: I have met some believers who use the whole idea of spiritual gifts as a cop-out to avoid getting involved in any uncomfortable works of service. For example: Harry has been a Christian for years and has still not identified his gift. Consequently, he doesn't really serve anybody. "I just don't know what my gift is," Harry explains. But Harry needs to plunge into action if he is to discover his gift. As he tries this way and that to make life better for folks around him, Harry's "gift" will eventually become obvious.

Beware of Dangerous Recruiters

We must beware of guilt-motivating zealots who think up programs then recruit square pegs into round holes, to keep their pet programs running. Beware of a pitch that sounds something like this, "People who don't teach Sunday school, don't really love kids." Or, "Those who really love lost souls will join our Tuesday-night witnessing team."

If I push my pet project and gobble up "recruits" whether gifts fit tasks or not, I am most definitely not treating people the way Jesus treated people. In fact, my insistence may even thwart God's plans and waste the gifts of others.

Each person is meant to do the work for which God designed him or her. "From him the whole body...grows and builds itself up...*as each part does its work*" (Eph. 4:16). The body of Christ has no extra, dispensable, vestigial organs. The body grows best when every person—not just some—uses his or her gifts!

God gives to every church all the gifts needed to do what God expects that church to do. He probably does not expect a community of believers to do things for which he has not supplied the gifts. But when each Christian in the body has identified his or her gift and is using that gift faithfully, the result is not only morale-building and fulfilling to each member of the body, but also powerfully effective in the Kingdom.

When Each Part Works

A report out of Phoenix a few years back demonstrates the power of spiritual gifts working together in harmony. Stephanie and Teena had never met each other, even though they lived in the same suburban Phoenix apartment complex and worked in the same downtown office building. They lived in two very different worlds. Stephanie was a legal secretary on the fourteenth floor and a genuine Christian. Teena, a friendly but thoroughly secular person, worked as a cocktail waitress in the mezzanine bar. Then came the energy crunch that started Stephanie and Teena carpooling daily from apartment building to office building, resulting in a close friendship between them.

Some weeks into their friendship, Teena observed, "Stephanie, something seems different about you! You seem to trust people. You expect good things to happen. You have lots of neat friends. The people you work with tell me that you never bad-mouth anybody—not even your overbearing boss. And they tell me you always pull more than your share of work. You trust men. You expect people to stay married. Tell me, what's your secret?"

Stephanie stammered at first. "Well, er...I don't want to sound like a holy Joe or anything, but if you see good stuff in my life, it's likely because I'm a Christian."

"So what's a Christian?"

"It's a...someone who follows Jesus Christ."

"How do you get to be one?"

"Well I, I don't know exactly how to tell you. But if you have some time Thursday night, come over for dinner, and I'll invite Sandra too. She's the one who explained it to me. I'll bet she can explain it to you too."

So Sandra, who had gifts of evangelism, taught Teena how to

become a Christian—and Teena accepted Christ. For the Sunday of her baptism, she sent out silver-embossed invitations to all of her friends, mostly clientele at the bar. Teena was streetwise and tough, but likeable too. So her friends said, "Hey, if it's for Teena, whatever it is—hog killing, bar mitzvah, birthday, baptism—we'll be there!"

And they came. Several pews full! Joking about the roof caving in because *they* were in church.

Meanwhile, Jennifer, another of Stephanie's Christian friends who had gifts of hospitality, sent out silver-embossed invitations to Teena's guest list, inviting them all to her house for a reception honoring Teena. Stephanie and Jennifer also invited Sandra and Stella, who had teaching gifts, and Fred, who had gifts of encouragement. Plus several other Christian friends.

When Teena's guests went from the baptism to the reception, God worked in this gift mix. Within the next year and a half, more than a dozen of Teena's friends accepted Jesus and sent out silver-embossed invitations to their baptisms, followed by Jennifer's receptions.

> "I DON'T WANT TO SOUND LIKE A HOLY JOE OR ANYTHING, BUT IF YOU SEE GOOD STUFF IN MY LIFE, IT'S LIKELY BECAUSE I'M A CHRISTIAN."

Questions: Who actually led Teena and her friends to Christ? Did Stephanie fail because she was not the one who actually taught Teena? Should Sandra feel guilty because she didn't actually baptize her? When the others became Christians, should Jennifer, Fred, and the gang feel left out because they neither witnessed, evangelized, nor baptized? Of course not! In Jesus' plan, every one of these

Christians played well his or her position on this soul-winning team. Each exercised his or her gift in a synergism, through which God met the needs of each new Christian at just the right time. And each found fulfillment in doing what God had designed him or her to do. As each part works properly, the body builds itself up in love (Eph. 4:16).

Jesus sat on a hill with his circle of followers gathered around him. He drew out the unique gift of each one, blended the gifts of all together, and created a mix that served and saved a multitude. He still does.

Creative Touch

Discover and use the unique gift God has given you
and help draw the God-given gifts out of others.

Thought Questions

1. Do you know your own spiritual gift? How did you discover it, or how will you?

2. What do you do best in the Lord's Kingdom? Is that also what you enjoy? Could that be your gift?

3. Have you felt God leading you toward other gifts? How do you know? What do these nudgings feel like?

Action Questions

1. What service need lies in your path right now that likely should be done by you—whether you feel gifted for it or not? When will you do it?

2. What specific ministry are you doing now that doesn't really fit your gifts? What specific ministry can replace it? What steps can you take today to move toward serving by gift?

3. Who can you help to find their gift? How? When?

Chapter 10

THE JESUS style

FINDING POWER WHERE YOU LEAST EXPECT IT

Now look at what he's gotten us into. We kids never could figure out our big brother.

Mom and Dad tell strange stories about the night he was born. And ever since he was twelve, he hasn't seemed exactly normal. At times we thought he was a bit touched in the head. But at other times he held us spellbound. He did some amazing things. Miracles, actually. Drew huge crowds everywhere. And the things he said! We felt both mystified and scared to death. But since he set the whole countryside buzzing, we were all proud of him. We enjoyed the attention that spilled over onto us. He seemed headed for the top.

Earlier this week we tried to bring him with us to the festival. "Everybody that is anybody will be there," we told him. "Sure, it's a religious gathering, but it's also a public relations bonanza." We knew our brother had the stuff to blow the doors off this crowd of big shots. We just knew this would be his big break. Walk in and wow this bunch, and the whole nation would be eating out of his hand. And ours. So we told him, "Here's your big chance. You'll never amount to much hanging around this dump.

Take your tricks to the city, now, at festival time. Show your stuff under the bright lights."

But he rattled off some riddle and stayed behind. So now he shows up—in the middle of a mad crowd. No bodyguards, and no miraculous tricks. And listen to him. Can you believe what he is saying to those big shots? Doesn't he know who they are? Why, that loony brother of ours is liable to...that is...he might actually get himself killed.

I'm outta here.

When the Jewish Feast of Tabernacles was near, Jesus'
brothers said to him, "You ought to leave here and go to
Judea, so that your disciples may see the miracles you do.
No one who wants to become a public figure acts in secret.
Since you are doing these things, show yourself to the
world." For even his own brothers did not believe in him.

Therefore Jesus told them, "The right time for me has
not yet come; for you any time is right. The world cannot
hate you, but it hates me because I testify that what it does
is evil. You go to the Feast. I am not yet going up to this
Feast, because for me the right time has not yet come."
Having said this, he stayed in Galilee.

However, after his brothers had left for the Feast, he
went also, not publicly, but in secret. Now at the Feast the
Jews were watching for him and asking, "Where is that
man?"

Among the crowds there was widespread whispering
about him. Some said, "He is a good man."

Others replied, "No, he deceives the people." But no one
would say anything publicly about him for fear of the
Jews.

John 7:2–13

THE JESUS style

FINDING POWER WHERE YOU LEAST EXPECT IT

His brothers thought Jesus needed to be brought up to speed in the science of public relations. He was too timid, too camera shy. He spent too much time alone. He didn't know how to set up a photo opportunity. He didn't see the power of pulling strings. He didn't drop names, kiss babies, or polish apples. His timing was off. His stage presence dull. He lacked tact. He didn't know how to play the crowd, manipulate the media, or grab headlines. He didn't seem to understand that if you're going to be a winner, you've got to operate from a position of strength.

So Jesus' brothers decided to coach him a bit. A feast day was coming! This would offer a great opportunity for a superstar to shine and strut. Lots of people. Lots of action. The network cameras would be rolling, and anyone on his way to the top couldn't afford to pass up a chance like this.

"You ought to leave here and go to Judea, so that your disciples may see the miracles you do. No one who wants to become a public figure acts in secret. Since you are doing these things, show yourself to the world" (John 7:3–4).

In other words, "C'mon, brother! Flex your muscles. Flash your pearly whites. Razzle-dazzle 'em, Jesus. That's the way to win the world."

Sounds familiar, right? Don't we still say that you need your hand on the throttle if you're going to move down the track? You need to know which buttons to push and which arms to twist. It is very possible that if Jesus were here today, we would give him the same advice.

Can you imagine one of our political handlers or celebrity managers giving Jesus a few pointers?

"To begin with, Jesus, you've got to get out of this one-horse town. You'll never get anywhere with Nazareth as your base. It's too ethnically typecast and primitive. So is Jerusalem, for that matter. We'll get you to Rome. Work on your accent. Get you some new clothes. (Heaven knows you could use them.) We'll build you a whole new image.

> YOU NEED YOUR HAND ON THE THROTTLE IF YOU'RE GOING TO MOVE DOWN THE TRACK.

"And these guys you hang out with? They stay here. There isn't much room in the Roman power structure for a bunch of hicks who smell like fish. We'll round you up some guys who'll give you some class.

"One other thing: If there is anything to this stuff about being born in a stable, play that down. It hurts your credibility.

"We've got a lot of work to do, Jesus. A lot of polishing and shining. By the way, have you ever heard of Madison Avenue? Ratings? George Gallop? Sound bytes? Letterman, Leno, and *Larry King Live?*"

The reason Jesus' brothers wanted Jesus to operate from a position of strength is clear: Scripture says "his own brothers did not believe" (John 7:5). You mean they were atheists? Well, no. They were religious, all right. No doubt they believed God existed. But they didn't understand that their brother was God come into our world to be a servant and to finally go to a cross.

John 5:44 hits this same point with a hammer blow: "How can you believe if you accept praise from one another, yet make no effort to obtain the praise that comes from the only God?" So in other words, to believe is to give glory to God and to seek his approval above all else.

When we manipulate events in order to be praised by people, we are not believing in God; we are believing in ourselves. And when push comes to shove, whatever gets us praise from people (votes, prestige, success, security, power) will win out time after time. How can we say we really believe, if the approval of our fellows matters more to us than the smile of heaven?

Interacting with People

Jesus Was Vulnerable

A fundamental flaw in the brothers' assumptions warped their counsel: "If you want to become a public figure..." Jesus had no desire to become a public figure. Where did his brothers get that idea? The kind of Messiah they believed in was not the Messiah Jesus would be. They couldn't see that Jesus wasn't aiming to impress people. His agenda was not visibility, fame, or clout. So his approach bewildered his brothers. It was 180 degrees off their course. For although Jesus was Lord, he chose to operate from a position of vulnerability, even of weakness. No puffed-up, Madison-Avenue image here.

Some seem to think that vulnerability and Christianity don't mix. "A Christian should always maintain his or her dignity," they advise. "Christians should never show their emotions lest they appear soft. Camouflage your weaknesses. Present your best profile. Don't allow yourself to get into a situation where you come off looking silly. Always be in charge of yourself and in control of the situation. Never let 'em see you sweat!"

Can you imagine our Lord hiding his emotions in order to impress the crowds? Not really. But you can imagine him removing his clothes and washing the apostles' feet. You can imagine him brushing away a tear with one hand while touching a leper with the other. You can imagine him burying his face in his hands in front of Lazarus's tomb. And you can imagine him redfaced and furious as he roared through the tables of the moneychangers in the Temple.

That's vulnerability.

Jesus made himself totally available and absolutely vulnerable— even to the enemy. What's more, he flung down inflammatory words before them, without the protection of any prestigious group behind him and with no bodyguards around him. He boldly asked, "Why are you trying to kill me?" No sham here. Jesus made himself absolutely vulnerable. That is how he operated. Eight hundred years earlier, the prophets said he would:

> He grew up before him like a tender shoot,
>> and like a root out of dry ground.
> He had no beauty or majesty to attract us to him,
>> nothing in his appearance that we should desire him.

He was despised and rejected by men,

a man of sorrows, and familiar with suffering.

Like one from whom men hide their faces

he was despised, and we esteemed him not. (Isa. 53:2–3)

Jesus made himself vulnerable—operating from a position of weakness, not of strength (John 12:44). And today he calls us to follow! To deny self, take up a cross, and follow!

Jesus Was Authentic

One word describes the way people perceived Jesus as he walked among them: *authentic*. He was accused of being a lot of things, but he was never accused of not being himself. In fact, to the contrary, people were amazed at how genuine and candid he was.

With Jesus, what folks saw was what they got. He presented his genuine self with his true values. There is not a hint in the New Testament of Jesus' putting up a front. He didn't try to put a "spin" on the humble facts. He neither disguised nor capitalized on his humble birth. He was never embarrassed to be seen with his mother, nor did he try to sanctify her. He didn't want titles, like "Rabbi" or "Teacher." He wasn't too dignified to play with children or too holy to eat with the pimps and prostitutes on the other side of the tracks. He didn't jockey for the head table. Nor was he the first to roar away from a traffic light.

If authenticity were a portrait, it would be painted in earthy tones. This is how I picture the authentic qualities of Jesus: honesty, the shade of a brown log cabin; simplicity, a bright, springish green; sincerity in a tone of sunset gold that invites friendship;

acceptance of an ocean blue that brings memories like the cool breeze of salty air.

Genuineness doesn't need glitzy neon colors that flash with overstatement and disguise. There is no need for blistering yellows or roaring purples to cover up the real self. Courageous authenticity allows a person to stand alone. Crutches made of professions, possessions, and designer clothes are thrown out; the real person remains. No games. No charades. No fronts.

> NO GAMES.
> NO CHARADES.
> NO FRONTS.

Problem is, these days we are tempted to overstate who we are because glitz markets better than genuineness, advertising better than authenticity. Shortly before his death, Dean Martin commented on the glitz of Hollywood: "Everything is a sham, a racket, from sex to singing to cultural respectability. You're born, you die, and in between you somehow delude yourself into thinking some of it means something."[1]

A lot of people see the world this way. Maybe that's why it's so refreshing to meet a person who is not obsessed with impressing you, who isn't trying to manipulate you. We just feel better around someone whose self-image isn't wrapped up in what he drives or who she knows or what he owns, much less in whom he or she controls.

People must have felt refreshed when they encountered Jesus. They might not have agreed with him or understood him, but they could never say he didn't give them the unvarnished truth about himself.

When Jesus' friend John was an old man, he began a letter reminding his readers of Jesus' authenticity: "That which was from the beginning, which we have heard, which we have seen with our eyes, which we have looked at and our hands have touched—this we proclaim concerning the Word of life" (1 John 1:1).

"We have seen God!" John declares. "He has been here among us and we have seen him. But God didn't disguise himself in bright lights nor did he hide on a mountain. He was in our midst. He wore diapers. He burped. He sweated. He ate with us. He talked our language. He touched us. And we touched him."

Jesus didn't take his brothers' advice because it wasn't his style. It wasn't who he was—and is. It went against Jesus' whole nature to be anything but himself. Besides, he was more interested in relationship with us than intimidation over us.

So instead of roaring to the Jerusalem feast in a limousine surrounded by hoopla and flag waving, Jesus waited. He waited until he could slip into the city quietly. No trumpets. No fanfare. He didn't announce his presence and then bolster it with, "I'm the fellow who walked on water and fed the five thousand—so you better listen up." *Au contraire.* He walked in a side door and simply began to teach.

Mirroring His Style

Jesus not only personally walked a vulnerable road, he taught his friends to walk that way as well.

The apostle Paul picked up on this, "Christ Jesus came into the world to save sinners—of whom I am the worst" (1 Tim. 1:15). That was not merely Paul's technique. Nor was it a communication device to diminish the talking distance between himself and "ordinary mortals." This was Paul's genuine lifestyle. His honest estimation of himself. Like Jesus, he refused to pretend he was something more than he was simply to gain advantages or credibility.

Listen again to Paul: "When I came to you, brothers, I did not come with eloquence or superior wisdom…" (1 Cor. 2:1). Now watch this: "I came to you in *weakness and fear,* and with much *trembling.* My message and my preaching were not with wise and persuasive words, but with a demonstration of the Spirit's power, so that your faith might not rest on men's wisdom, but on *God's power*" (1 Cor. 2:3–5). And Paul's vulnerability was his strength! From a human standpoint, he was defeated, in prison, under threat of the death penalty—yet Paul transformed the world.

Or consider Peter. If anyone had a reason for some boasting, Peter did. Skim his résumé:

- three years personal training under the Son of God

- personal friend of Jesus

- present at the transfiguration, the Garden of Gethsemane, and the crucifixion

- walked on water

- received the gift of speaking in other languages

- personally commissioned by God to carry the gospel into all parts of the world

- worker of various miracles and cures

- witness to visions

- writer of two New Testament letters

Some bio, huh? Can you imagine a long-ball hitter like that being introduced to speak at a Christian conference? My, the introduction would crowd the message off the clock! That kind of experience should be broadcast loudly in order to enhance credibility, right?

Apparently not for Peter! When the opportunity came to list off his qualifications, he chose instead to write simply, "Simon Peter, a servant and apostle of Jesus Christ" (2 Pet. 1:1).

The Style of the World

In some quarters, we modern North American believers have developed the dangerous habit of depending on our own power and talents for Kingdom business. After all, this is how you get ahead in most other fields. It works, right? But if you follow the advice of the power brokers, you will quickly find yourself out on a limb. Jesus warned his followers:

> You know that the rulers of the Gentiles lord it over them, and their high officials exercise authority over them. Not so with you. Instead, whoever wants to become great among you must be your servant, and whoever wants to be first must be your slave—just as the Son of Man did not come to be served, but to serve, and to give his life as a ransom for many. (Matt. 20:25–28)

But in spite of his clear warning, the show-'em-your-stuff mentality sometimes overflows into the church. In fact, sometimes one of the hardest places to find authenticity is among "religious" people. Before you dismiss this brash assertion, consider some clues to our position-of-strength, project-a-good-image, and never-let-'em-see-you-sweat mentality.

Cover Up

For one thing, we tend to *cover our flaws.* We dress sharp. We smell good. Plastic smiles sparkle in our church pews. Neat leather Bibles lay open on laps. We nod at the right places, stand at the right moments, and bow at the appropriate times. My, we look nice.

But we wonder how many broken hearts beat painfully beneath our new suits. How much anxiety is camouflaged by makeup?

What would happen in your church if you had a dress-like-you-really-feel Sunday? How many would show up in new clothes? In all probability, very few. Some folks might come clothed in white hospital robes, peeling off bandages, baring their wounds for treatment. Others would be draped in mourning clothes. Still others might sit in sackcloth and ashes.

Maybe the idea wouldn't be all bad. Real spiritual healing only comes through this kind of honesty: "Confess your sins to each other and pray for each other so that you may be healed" (James 5:16).

The church is strongest when it rings truest. Can you imagine cute pep rally songs in the catacomb assemblies of the first century? Did the leaders, stumbling through dark corridors with candles in their hands, get hung up on clerical image or public relations strategies for moving to a position of strength? Can you envision the apostles babbling empty religious clichés and wearing pompous clergy clothes?

Of course not. The Christian movement roared across the civilized world, clothed in integrity, not image. The best growth rates were the years without legal recognition or social clout—even years of persecution—because God blessed authentic faith! Later, after the Edict of Constantine, when the church received legal status and began to jockey for the support of political power, the Christian movement began to lose its steam.

Charisma

In some circles these days, leaders tend to rely on *ministry by charisma.* We want preachers who can wow the audience. Let Christ be represented by a real charmer, someone who can bring in the crowds and entertain the masses. Of course, there is nothing wrong with utilizing God-given gifts of communication. But there is something seriously wrong, maybe even idolatrous, in attempting to replace God's Holy Spirit with the force of human personality or scholarship or reputation or…!

Position

We sometimes operate as if we expect Kingdom growth through *political posturing.* We want to headline Christians who can impress. Wouldn't it be great if the governor were a part of our church? Wouldn't it be something if we could get a movie star to testify at our services? Or how about a former porn publisher?

In Canada, the premier of the province lived in our city, and we became superficially acquainted with him and his family. I remember waking in the night, fantasizing that the premier of British Columbia might become part of our little church plant. What a boost that would give us! We would have some prestige in the community, and then people would want to be part of our church!

WE SOMETIMES OPERATE AS IF WE EXPECT KINGDOM GROWTH THROUGH *POLITICAL POSTURING.*

Truth is, all people need the gospel. But God doesn't need just the influential to carry his message. If, in times past, he has succeeded in communicating through donkeys and tornadoes, he can probably use ordinary Janes and Joes like you and me. And what real spiritual benefit would there be in attending a church simply because the premier went there?

Scholarship

Some of us may have attempted to wow people with our erudition—*intimidation by information.* We try to blow people away with our Bible knowledge. We fire off a barrage of biblical bullets from six feet above criticism, quoting our repertoire of verses and packaged answers, ready-made for any situation. We anticipate objections, ask leading questions, close with strong emotion. We *sell* Jesus—which may leave the poor, intimidated soul saying yes to our pitch without really saying yes to Jesus. There is a vast difference between low sales resistance and a holy hunger for God.

Professionalism

Some may also at times feel tempted to trust in *religious professionalism.* Manipulation. Climbing the ecclesiastical ladder can become an appealing workout routine for church leaders. Titles, credentials, speaking invitations, growth statistics, published books, and the like become toeholds to higher rungs on the ladder, while the crowd marvels at "how mightily God is using Brother Big-Shot." (Such accolades leave some faithful servants in the crowd feeling personally useless to Christ because they themselves are so "ordinary" by comparison.)

Constellations of these power moves can converge to create a dense and intimidating network of *professionalism* in church circles, leading us farther away from the people in the streets and imprisoning these professionals in offices, conference rooms, libraries, and airplanes. Once-effective servants are slowly strangled by clerical collars and cluttered calendars.

What a stark contrast between the prophet in the Bible and the religious professional in the limelight. Professionalism runs counter to the heart of Jesus. I am convinced that the more professional I long to be, the more artificial I become.

There is no such thing as professional childlikeness. There is no professional tenderheartedness. There is no professional panting after God.

Years ago, I read an article that launched the following thoughts. (In fact, some of the following lines contain direct quotes, but alas, I cannot recover the source, but the ideas are too good to leave out. Whoever you are, I'm indebted to you.) In essence, the elusive author said: Prophets are needed more urgently than professionals— prophets who deny themselves rather than professionals who exalt themselves. Prophets who are plain rather than professionals who are polished. Prophets who may get stoned rather than professionals who get etched in stone. Prophets walking with Jesus, who hunger for God in prayer and who weep over sins and injustices and suffering.

Prophets! Not slick professionals with Teflon exteriors that slough off the messy, painful side of life. God draws us toward the holiness of heaven. Is there professionalism in that?

The world sets the agenda for the professional man, but the spiritual person follows God's agenda. The new wine of Jesus bursts the old wineskins of professionalism. We don't need professionalism; we need a holy hunger for God.

Of Strength and Weakness

We cannot cover our flaws forever. And if we rely on charisma, position, scholarship, and professionalism, we will quickly stumble into several booby traps. For one, such a pose is impossible to hold for very long. For another, while the pose lasts, it intimidates those who buy into it. Such a false front definitely impedes intimacy and inspires no one. And most importantly, it isn't Jesus' style!

The Weakness of Strength

Do you sense the liabilities?

One huge weakness of strength is this: When we hold any kind of power over another person (be it physical, positional, or even psychological), we are never sure how genuine our relationship with that person is. A wealthy friend of mine, in a moment of candor, once told me, "I never know for sure who my real friends are because everybody fawns over me and then wants something." We never really know how authentic our relationship is with anyone who stands in awe of us or fears us or is beholden to us or wants to use us. Only in vulnerability and openness do we really know where we stand. Only then can we trust a relationship to be real.

A second weakness of strength is that when I operate from a position of power or psychological advantage over someone, I rob that individual of personhood. I subtly diminish that person's significance and make him or her a mere tool of my attempts to control. But God doesn't operate that way! Jesus came as a servant, and he died on a cross.

A third weakness of strength is idolatry. When I attempt to control from a position of power, God gets dethroned and I take charge.

Finally, our attempts to operate from a position of strength can ultimately lead to depletion, even to meltdown, of influence. We saw this happen in the 1992 Texas state elections. Former State Railroad Commissioner Lena Guerrero, who began her campaign with a strong lead and had done a good job at her previous state appointment, lost the race dismally. Investigative reporters learned that she pretended to have graduated from the University of Texas and to have been a member of Phi Beta Kappa honor scholastic society. But the truth came out that she hadn't graduated at all. In fact, she had flunked a number of courses including Mexican Americans in the Southwest, Texas Legislature, and Readings in Government.[2] Apparently Mrs. Guerrero couldn't resist the temptation to present an image larger than life. Few people who want positions of power can. Why? They feel they need to operate from a position of more strength than they believe they have!

How sad to think that we need something bigger than reality to do God's work.

Pause and think for a minute. How do those who know you best perceive you? Would you fit the description of a prophet or a professional? As authentic or artificial? You may want to evaluate yourself using the following questions:

- Do I try to project more strength or claim more power than I really have?

- Do I feel a need to communicate personal achievements in order to be a legitimate and comfortable player in a relationship?

- Do people around me feel that I will listen to them if they have a problem?

- What percentage of my time am I available to people who want to talk to me but who are not "useful" to me?

- Can I name a person who was served by me in the last few days?

The Strength of Weakness

On the opposite pole, What about the strength of weakness and vulnerability? Vulnerability brings a number of powerful pluses:

- vulnerability promotes honesty, thus
- vulnerability inspires trust, thus

- vulnerability lowers defenses, thus

- vulnerability melts hostility, thus

- vulnerability puts a listener at ease, and

- when we relinquish our position of strength, we become more teachable ourselves.

The bottom line is: Vulnerability forces us to be authentic!

That's how Jesus functioned. That was his style of interacting with people. Write this in stone: Authentic Christianity creates abiding faith. The real thing may not create flashing lights or blasting trumpets, but the long-term results are enormously substantial: a personal faith that can stand alone, free of crutches, makeup, or razzle-dazzle; an obedient trust in Jesus and nothing else!

Authenticity is refreshing. We can relax and avoid the mad scramble to cover for our mistakes. We need no longer feel stressed by our compulsion to impress people with our achievements because we realize that anything we have achieved is trash in comparison with God's gift. We feel no burden to drive the best or wear the latest because our self-image ultimately comes from God's assessment of us, not other people's.

Part of being authentic is knowing how to respond to criticism. My father used to tell me that when I am criticized—before I react—to ask myself if there is any truth to the criticism. If so, he told me, apologize and correct it. If upon reflection, I determine that the criticism isn't based on truth, then ask myself, *Why are those people criticizing me?*

- *Is it because they are misinformed?* If so, provide them with the facts.

- *Is it because they are hurting?* If so, they need love and compassion.

- *Is it because they are sick?* If so, they need ministry and prayer.

- *Is it because they are just plain wicked and mean?* If so, they are objects of evangelism.

Whatever the case, he said, "Don't be defensive." And finally, he told me, "Spend most of your coffee money on your biggest critics."

How to Get Real

If we truly want to touch people the way Jesus did, we must ask the questions: How do I become more authentic? If I have become too plastic in my relationships, what can I do?

Start with Your Heart

At least part of the answer seems almost too simple. Authenticity is the result of an unquenchable love for the Savior. Think about it.

If one loves Jesus with a whole heart, what room is left for self-protection and duplicity? None. If there is no self left, there is no need for self-promotion. The more we love the Master, the less we are concerned about self and the more authentic we are. The more we are consumed with presenting the Savior, the less we feel the need to present ourselves.

Living authenticity, then, is a fruit of full relationship with Jesus. But in this world, full relationship with Christ is always a direction we are heading, not a place we have arrived. And consistent, accountable relationships with other believers fuel our momentum in that direction. Paradoxically, the most authentic I can be is to honestly admit my "inauthenticity" to my fellow believers and to team up with them as we monitor each other's progress.

Pay the Pain Price

We will never be authentic unless we are willing to pay the price. Authenticity appears most fully in those whom life has genuinely broken, and this is disturbing. Vulnerability means we may get taken advantage of, even hurt deeply. Jesus was—many times—long before he went to the cross, which is why he is said to be a "man of sorrows, and familiar with suffering" (Isa. 53:3).

We need not be surprised that we, his followers, sometimes hurt. At an earlier stage of my Christian walk, I believed that Christians *might* suffer deep hurt if they practiced servant-heartedness. I am now firmly convinced that suffering is inevitable. Suffering is the very means by which some of the most significant "people touching" is done. In fact, the most pivotal service ever done took place six hours one Friday, when a man hung on a cross in the dark and screamed, "My God, why have you forsaken me?"

Dr. James Dittes calls ministry "grief work." In his book *When the People Say No,* he wrote:

> To grieve is to take two cups of coffee in the morning only to remember that one's wife is dead or separated and to have to put one cup back. To grieve is to wake up on a brilliant sunny morning with spontaneous, unbidden anticipation of playing golf that day only to be reminded instantly by heavy limbs that one has had a stroke and to close one's eyes now moist. To grieve is to pour one's energies for months and years into the struggle of a beleaguered family or marriage or teenager—standing by patiently and wisely and lovingly, and indeed making the crucial difference—only to have that group or couple or teenager having found them-

selves, shun you as a threatening enemy. After all, you know too many secrets.

Other people may experience only a few times in a long lifetime the grief of losing a crucial partner or the grief of a crucial promise broken by a parent or a teacher, absolutely trusted till then, or the grief of being jilted by a lover or divorced by a spouse or betrayed by a friend.

But a genuine ministering Christian experiences many such moments of grief. Indeed we may frequently experience all of these in the course of only one week.[3]

That's OK. It happened to Jesus first. The man of sorrows, acquainted with grief, operated on my soul and yours by totally allowing himself to be hated and rejected and killed. Sometimes joy and laughter can only be found at the bottom of a broken heart.

Three Words

We don't hear much out of Jesus' brothers after they gave Jesus their pep talk on public relations. And were it not for three special words written by Luke, the end of their story would remain a mystery. Luke, however, fills us in on the outcome—with just three words—three words that can easily pass unnoticed. Yet these words drive home the payoff of authenticity. Get your pen poised because you'll want to underline them.

You'll find them in the first chapter of Acts, verse 14. Luke has just listed the names of those who watched Jesus ascend to heaven and then gathered together to pray. Friends get first billing: Peter, John, James, and the other apostles. Of course, Mary too. Then Luke says:

"They all joined together constantly in prayer, along with the women and Mary the mother of Jesus, and *with his brothers*" (Acts 1:14).

There they are. The brothers of Jesus. They are the same ones who tried to coach Jesus into the winner's circle, who tried to position him for power; the same ones who wanted to help Jesus get to the top. But now they have seen him front and center—hanging on a cross. Totally vulnerable. Totally helpless. Yet totally powerful and totally victorious. The same brothers who didn't believe in him *now believe!*

A Place of Weakness

Although he is the ruler of the kings of the earth, Jesus chose not to operate from a position of strength, but from a place of weakness and vulnerability. "The Son of Man did not come to be served, but to serve." He did not come to promote himself, but to "give his life as a ransom for many" (Mark 10:45).

The following poem from an unknown author gives expression to the bared soul of vulnerability and reveals its reward:

It's my soul lying there.

You don't know what a soul is?

You think it's some flimsy, sheet-like thing

that you can see through

and that floats on air.

It's my soul lying there.

You don't know what a soul is?

Well, that's my soul lying there.

Remember the time that I giggled and

laughed too much and embarrassed

myself in the group?

I put my soul on the line.

That's my soul lying there.

Remember the time that I got angry

and out of control and made

a fool of myself?

Well, I was putting my soul

on the line that time too.

That's my soul lying there.

You can pick it up if you want to.

It'll bruise and turn rancid

like an old banana if you manhandle it.

I think it'll go away if you ignore it.

But if you'll put your soul there

beside it, you might find love.

We might even find God.

We might even find God.

Your prayer to imitate Jesus' style might sound something like mine: Oh, hope of all the ends of the earth and of the farthest seas, please make me real and authentic, clean through. Teach me to depend on you and you only for my sense of worth and security. Deliver me from the low, maneuvering, manipulating, and contriving trends of our times. Banish professionalism from my presence and put in its place passion and prayer, poverty of spirit, rigorous study of holy things, white-hot devotion to Jesus Christ, utter indifference to material gain, and untiring labor to rescue the lost. Amen.

Creative *Touch*

As you interact with people, imitate the vulnerability and authenticity of our Savior and find his strength in your weakness.

Thought Questions

1. Why didn't Jesus want to impress people with his style? How should we follow his example?

2. In what ways have you seen the show-'em-your-stuff mentality come into the church? Into your life?

3. Do you feel more like a prophet or a professional? Why?

Action Questions

1. What does "strength in vulnerability" mean for you? Do you have it? What step can you take today to cultivate it?

2. In what situation you are facing now have you been tempted to operate from a position of strength? What concrete steps can you take toward vulnerability?

Chapter 11

RESTORING personhood

BALANCING LAW AND LOVE

Aren't all men interested in the same thing? Not that I minded, of course. Until! Until that horrible, wonderful day. I guess I should have expected to be caught. But the possibility never crossed my mind until the door burst open and these high-and-mighty types from down around the Temple pulled me right out of what's-his-name's arms and dragged me out the door with scarcely time to grab my coat.

They forced me into a circle of gawking men. Then they stopped and looked around for the carpenter and shoved me right up in his face. At first, I couldn't bear to raise my head, but when I finally looked into his eyes, he looked back at me in the most striking way, totally different from the way any man had ever looked at me up close before.

Suddenly, everybody was shouting at once, demanding that this north-country carpenter pass the sentence of adultery on me. At first, I was utterly humiliated. Then, when I realized they had deliberately left my man behind, I was roaring mad. That is, until both humiliation and anger froze into terror when I heard, "Stone her until she is dead."

What happened next is all a blur. The carpenter said

nothing. Just knelt and started writing with his finger in the dirt. The crowd kept demanding that he sentence me. He stood again and looked at them, in that same strange way he had first looked at me. Then he spoke something softly to the crowd of men and knelt again.

But Jesus went to the Mount of Olives. At dawn he appeared again in the temple courts, where all the people gathered around him, and he sat down to teach them. The teachers of the law and the Pharisees brought in a woman caught in adultery. They made her stand before the group and said to Jesus, "Teacher, this woman was caught in the act of adultery. In the Law Moses commanded us to stone such women. Now what do you say?" They were using this question as a trap, in order to have a basis for accusing him.

But Jesus bent down and started to write on the ground with his finger. When they kept on questioning him, he straightened up and said to them, "If any one of you is without sin, let him be the first to throw a stone at her." Again he stooped down and wrote on the ground.

At this, those who heard began to go away one at a time, the older ones first, until only Jesus was left, with the woman still standing there.

John 8:1–9

Chapter 11

RESTORING personhood
BALANCING LAW AND LOVE

How would you like to listen to a kettledrum solo for a couple of hours? Boom, boom, boom. A few minutes? OK, but even the best of musicians can get only so much variety out of this mama of percussion instruments. "Not a kettledrum," you say, "but give me two hours with the soaring soprano of the flute. That would be sweet to the ear." Ahh, now that is music—for a while. In fact, there are very few instruments that played solo can sustain our interest for long periods of time. The long-term attraction of a good orchestra is not its solos, but its symphony. Music moves us when it delicately balances and blends, say, the melodious trumpet with the thundering tuba and the compelling clarinet with the subtle strings of the violin.

Now move that balance principle from the concert hall to the kitchen. A delicious meal essentially includes a balanced blend of the sweet and the sour, the strong and the subtle, the predictable and the exotic. A good chef mixes ingredients (like flour, raw eggs, or lard, yuk!) that by themselves are undesirable; but when paired with the right pan-partners, they become mouth-watering, finger-licking dishes (like, say, strawberry shortcake or pecan pie!).

World-class athletes also know the value of balance. They blend strength with style, speed with control, and training with rest. It takes a synchronized spectrum of muscles, coordinated correctly, to throw farther, run faster, or jump higher than the competition and bring home the gold. So a key secret in sports, cuisine, or music is *balance!*

To no one is balance more important than to a person attempting to honor God. The King James Version translates the words of the wise man: My son, forget not my law; but let thine heart keep my commandments: For length of days, and long life, and peace, shall they add to thee. Let not mercy and truth forsake thee (Prov. 3:1–3).

Balance. Balance of law and heart, mercy and truth.

Like the conductor, the chef, and the athlete, the follower of Jesus must carefully balance the ingredients of faith. It's crucial, not just for you or me, but also for those we come in contact with.

One aim of a balanced spiritual life is to treat other people with the right touch of spiritual balance—like Jesus did. Coordinating praise and correction. Sprinkling doctrine with spontaneity. Knowing when to forgive and when to rebuke. That is balance.

But it's tricky. Sometimes we are so bent on being right with God that we misuse people. And sometimes we are so afraid of hurting people that we water down the will of God. Some of us are so bent on truth that we forget mercy, others so tenderhearted that we forget truth.

Tip this delicate spiritual scale, and we may tumble headlong into one extreme or another. Traditions begin to outweigh effectiveness or pragmatism upstages biblical truth. Sometimes people get sacrificed on the altar of doctrinal purity; at other times we give away the store of divine truth in the name of being people-sensitive.

Is balance possible? Is it realistic for us to attempt to deal with people in both grace and truth?

This question is a key one, not only for individual Christ-followers, but also for churches that are serious about being obedient to the Scriptures. When do you allow divorce, and when do you prohibit it? When do you discipline, and when do you let go and forgive? When do you overlook sin in the name of patience, and when do you confront it in the name of purity? When are we to be held accountable, and when do we need empathy?

Jesus' Balancing Act

To learn the secrets of the proper balance, we look, of course, to the Master. Watch his balance as he encounters several kinds of sin and several extenuating circumstances in one chapter of Scripture—John 8. The lead players in this drama represent the two extremes: overzealous religious leaders determined to protect the institution and enforce the law contrasted with a sinful woman in desperate need of grace. Between them stands Jesus. He extends his hands in both directions and offers this principle: Beware of a view of the law that hurts people.

> TO LEARN THE SECRETS OF THE PROPER BALANCE, WE LOOK, OF COURSE, TO THE MASTER.

This principle was dramatically played out in the busy courtyard of the Temple. The city was just beginning to stir that morning when Jesus descended from the Mount of Olives. Dew moistened the grass and crowing roosters split the silence. Early risers were leaving their homes and going to work. While merchants opened their shops, children left for school, and blacksmiths fired their forges.

All around town, people were buzzing about the strange man from Galilee. Yesterday he had shocked everyone by asserting, "If anyone is thirsty, let him come to me and drink. Whoever believes in me, as the Scripture has said, streams of living water will flow from within him" (John 7:37–38).

Animated controversy broke out,

"What kind of man would say such things?"

"He must be a prophet."

"I think he is the Messiah."

"Are you crazy? He is an imposter!"

No wonder, then, that the moment Jesus entered the Temple court, a crowd encircled him. The Master sat down and began to teach.

The Prosecution

He was soon interrupted, however, as another crowd erupted into the Temple court. It was a small mob. An angry mob. They marched with a confident fierceness, eyes burning with religious fervor. They were elegantly dressed and looked powerful: well-trimmed beards, flowing robes, and colorful cords. National leaders. They were the Supreme Court, Vatican, and Congress of the Jewish people. Wealthy and powerful. Not accustomed to sharing the spotlight with anyone, especially a blue-collared carpenter. And no question about it, the teachings of this young carpenter threatened to topple them from prestigious positions. He must be stopped.

They shoved along a woman, half-dressed, disheveled, eyes wide with fear. She struck a stark contrast to those dragging her through the narrow streets. They were in power; she was the victim. They were many; she was alone. They were self-righteousness; she was humiliated.

How They Saw the Woman

No doubt the woman struggled to keep her balance as each arm was squeezed in the grip of a fast-walking Pharisee. Her pain made no difference to them: They viewed the lady as *expendable!*

She strained to gather her thoughts. It had all happened so quickly. The door had flown open so violently that it had ricocheted off the wall. In they had stormed. She barely had time to grab something to cover her nakedness before being yanked into the street. She noticed that, although she was heavily guarded, most of what they were saying was oddly centered on someone else. "Let's take this one to *him*. We'll show the people the imposter he really is."

We don't know much about this woman. Perhaps she was a young girl who had spent a passionate night with a boyfriend. Or maybe passion was her profession and some of her accusers were also some of her customers. Or it's possible that she was a good wife simply caught in a one-time wayward rendezvous. We don't know. But for all we don't know, one thing we do know for sure: She was not the point. She was only a hapless pawn in a vicious power move. The Pharisees had no more desire to see justice done than they did to kiss a Roman soldier. Their sole desire was to neutralize Jesus' growing influence, and this woman presented a perfect opportunity. They would trap him, and she was their bait.

How They Saw Jesus

Jesus was a *threat*. Folks flocked to him in droves. He had dared to say that their system was going to end. Jesus threatened their position, their money, their prestige, and their power. Jesus even threatened their peace of mind because his words probed the depths of their hearts. And if they allowed themselves to think about these things too much, they couldn't live with themselves.

Jesus was also a threat because he was reminding people of the purpose of the law. He was reinstating balance. He was demonstrating that any use of law or doctrine that did not help people grow closer to God was not from God. You can mark that down: Any would-be application of God's Word that does not serve the betterment of people is actually a misuse of God's Word.

The group stormed through the crowd of listeners, scattering them like doves. The woman was thrown at the seated Nazarene with a torrent of accusations.

"We pulled this woman out of bed with her lover," a sarcastic voice shouted. "The law says to kill her. What would you have us do?"

I can imagine the group of Pharisees smiling smugly to each other, proud of their craftiness. They had him now!

How They Saw the Law

As the woman looked around at her accusers, she saw a group of men so consumed that they saw everything from a grossly distorted perspective.

Above all, this woman's accusers saw the law as *useful*. They burned with one passion: to protect their position in the religious institution. The law served as a useful tool for their purposes. The law with which they were concerned, however, went beyond God's law. It was *their* law: a complicated web of traditions and dictates added and designed to control people. And to them, what they called the law was sacred. This complex system had accrued layer upon layer for generations. It was the glue that held their socioreligious system together, assuring their security, status, and identity. This law was a club used to beat people into submission, especially helpless victims. And at this moment, the law was useful as a means of getting rid of this man Jesus in order to maintain control. It was their shears with which to clip the wings of this upstart Galilean who was soaring out of hand. So for these Pharisees, the law had become more important than people. Especially this person taken in adultery.

Now, the *actual* law of God was something else again. God originally designed his law to regulate the lives of human beings for their own greater good and God's greater glory. Put simply: The law was *for* man, not *against* him. As Jesus once put it, "The Sabbath was made for man, not man for the Sabbath" (Mark 2:27). The law was meant to expand the quality of life, not diminish it. For example, as Jesus explained on another occasion: "If any of you has a sheep and it falls into a pit on the Sabbath, will you not take hold of

> ANY WOULD-BE APPLICATION OF GOD'S WORD THAT DOES NOT SERVE THE BETTERMENT OF PEOPLE IS ACTUALLY A MISUSE OF GOD'S WORD.

it and lift it out? How much more valuable is a man than a sheep!" (Matt. 12: 11–12). Once again, Jesus was saying, "People are everything in God's scale of things."

Over in Mark's Gospel, when Jesus was asked, "What's the greatest commandment?" he answered unequivocally, "Love the Lord your God with all your heart and with all your soul and with all your mind and with all your strength.... Love your neighbor as yourself. *There is no commandment greater than these*" (Mark 12:30–31). The pinnacle of it all, he said, is to really love God and thus value people.

But the Pharisees were not interested in people, especially this poor person shivering before them.

How They Saw Sin

Since the Pharisees were consumed with protecting their position of power, they saw Jesus as a *threat,* the law as *useful,* and the woman as *expendable.* These accusing Pharisees also held a distorted view of sin. They saw sin as *inconsequential.*

If the Pharisees had been concerned with right and wrong, they would have looked for a way to help this woman find victory over sin. But her sin was beside the point and only important because it made her useful to them. Though God loved her enough to die for her, her enormous value as a human being completely escaped them. To them, she was merely a pawn in their game.

This woman's sin was, at most, only peripheral to their interests. In fact, the will of God was so peripheral that they could not see that their own sin was at least as great as the woman's. Of course adultery is disastrous. No question about that. But to dishonor God in the center of your heart, even attempt to use his law to trap his Son without any concern for people, has to be infinitely more damaging than adultery.

Don't miss the point. Whenever you find someone whose favorite pastime is finger pointing and whose favorite phrase is a thundering "The law of God says...," you can be sure of one thing: Some person at the other end of that pointing finger is about to get crushed. You can also be sure that somewhere behind all that thunder lurks, at best, a weak and stale relationship with God—if indeed there is any relationship at all. And at worst, as with this woman's accusers, a twisted view of law, a cheap view of people, and a warped view of God. Dangerous religion.

The Person Is Purpose

We can't afford to imitate the Pharisees, even inadvertently. We must be vigilant to apply God's Word in balanced ways and never, ever use law as a weapon against people. An imbalanced view of God inevitably leads us to mistreat people.

What happens to individuals can also happen to organizations, even to movements. Countless Christian movements have crystallized, outlived their time, and no longer serve their original purpose. Some are kept alive by loyalists who have forgotten that the only justifiable reason for the existence of any Christian movement is to take care of the people for whom Christ died. The minute a denomination, parachurch organization, university, or even a church stops caring for people, it is best to disband and begin afresh.

Why? Because that movement has become imbalanced. Pet peeves get bronzed. Some doctrines are dodged; others are defied. Institutions become sacred, and people become expendable. Scattered along beside the trail of religious history lie the bleached bones of person after person who got waylaid by self-appointed "institutional policemen" who knew how to accuse but forgot how to forgive and rescue. We start down this path the moment we stop seeing people as Jesus saw them.

The Defense

Having surveyed this scene through the eyes of the Pharisees, let us now turn back to John 8 and look at things through the eyes of Jesus.

As this woman searched around the circle of men, her eyes met no mercy. Face after face held furrowed brows and hard-set jaws. But when she found the tanned face of Jesus, she saw hope. In his eyes she read not accusation, but acceptance. His jaw was not set to condemn; rather his gaze reached out to comfort. In his silent glance, she sensed compassion and a better tomorrow.

Lean in now and notice carefully both what Jesus *did* and what he *did not* do.

Getting Her off the Hook

Immediately, Jesus *diverted the attention from the woman.* She was on cruel display before the gaping stares of the growing crowd. So Jesus' first concern was for her. He didn't get drawn into a religious argument about the woman. Rather, he knelt down and began to write in the sand. You can imagine all the eyes shifting and heads turning.

"What's he doing?"

"Is he picking up a rock?"

"I think he's praying."

No doubt the woman felt some relief, at least for a few moments, as she escaped the sea of eyes.

Nondefensive Defender

Second, Jesus *didn't fight back.* He might have considered demanding that the woman's lover be brought to trial. Or he could have debated that the law doesn't specify *how* a woman caught in adultery is to be killed (Lev. 20:10). Or he could have pointed out that the death sentence for adultery hadn't been enforced for centuries. But he didn't.

He took a far more difficult and creative tack. He wouldn't be seduced into going on the defensive because he didn't have anything to defend. He wasn't trying to protect his image or maintain control or score points. Rather, Jesus demonstrated how foolish and futile it is to get preoccupied with self-defense. When we are under attack for doing right, the best strategy is to continue on the high road of doing right and not wade into the quicksand of defensiveness.

We also see that Jesus was not bent on humiliating the woman's assailants, though they well deserved it. Remember, Jesus is always sensitive and helpful to people—to *all* people. In this case, both to the woman and to the Pharisees.

Again, Jesus is so creative in what he does. He baffles everyone. He kneels. And writes. And doesn't say a word.

The accusers didn't like the spooky silence. They kept repeating their question. Eventually Jesus stands and responded simply, "If any one of you is without sin, let him be the first to throw a stone at her" (John 8:7). Then he knelt down again. Silent once more.

Back in Their Court

How Jesus resisted the desire to burn these hypocrites on the spot can only be a testimony to his deity. For not only did he not punish or humiliate them, he gave them their personhood. "If any one of you…" He didn't point his finger to single out the accusers one by one and reveal their sins: *"You* are having an affair, and *you* cheated your business partner, and *you* haven't said a sincere prayer in a year." Rather, he *put the ball in their court* and simply said, "If any one of you is without sin, throw the first rock." And he knelt, not even glancing up to see who would

> JESUS' FIRST CONCERN WAS FOR HER.

205

walk away first. He didn't take down names so he could report them to the authorities. He didn't even check to see who was planning to throw rocks.

Jesus viewed all people in an astoundingly special way, including these accusers. In spite of what we don't like about them, they, too, are people whom God loves. Jesus saw that. Each person there was so valuable to him that he would soon die for them. So rather than put them on the spot, Jesus creatively put them on an inward journey. He left each man to wrestle with his own thoughts:

What about me?

Why am I really *here?*

What right do I honestly have to throw a rock at this woman?

What is really going on in my heart? Do I truly care about God?

Now honestly, what lies at the bottom of my resentment?

In my heart of hearts, why do I hate him like I do?

Maybe some began to reflect, "When I really think about it, instead of killing this carpenter—or whoever he is—I ought to be pleading to him for help."

The older men left first. No doubt, they'd met their share of shifty characters, from thugs to theologians to would-be prophets. And they sensed that this man was different. Perhaps, too, age brings us a more honest self-appraisal, an acute awareness of our own frailties. The longer we live, the more we discover how miserably we fail when left to our own devices.

See, over there a gray-whiskered chin drops to a heaving chest, maybe across the circle a tear slides down a weathered cheek. A pregnant silence settles over the crowd. A quiet so thick you can cut it with a knife. Finally, we hear the crunch of gravel underfoot as one man turns and walks away. Then another. We don't know how long it took that crowd to leave, but it must have seemed a century to that worried woman. I can't help but hope that, on their way out of the circle, some may have glanced into the woman's eyes and whispered, "Forgive me."

When they were gone, Jesus asked, "Where are they?" Jesus hadn't been keeping records. Eli, the adulterer, gone. Baruch, the liar, too, and Ben...

No, Jesus didn't watch the direction they walked; He had no desire to follow and hound them. He simply was not in the condemning business: "For God did not send his Son into the world to condemn the world, but to save the world through him" (John 3:17).

Jesus knew, too, that permanent change doesn't come without time, reflection, and self-examination. We are far more deeply convicted by self-recrimination than by the accusations of another. That's why Jesus dumped the questions back in the Pharisees' laps and left them to sort things out. He set them up for self-inventory. Instead of crossing theological swords, he simply led them to think!

With Music in Her Ears

J. Wallace Hamilton said that one day he heard horrible noises coming from the backyard. He peeked out his window to see two boys experimenting with an antique record player. Just for fun they had bored an extra hole in the old platter record, adjacent to the factory hole, but off-center. When they played the record on their off-center hole, instead of making music, it poured out a horrible cacophony of dissonant squawks and screeches. However, when they picked up the record and plopped it down on the hole in the center, the old platter filled the air with a harmonic symphony of beautiful music.

Life is like that. When we attempt to live life with self at the center rather than God, our hearts become flooded with disharmony and discord. Ignoring God's design for our lives and making up our rules for the game is what the Bible calls sin!

But when we turn and live life with him at the center, things fit. Then we can hope to find harmony and beauty in life.

The devil must take special delight in tipping Christians off-balance. Some of us "religious" people seem prone toward extreme and imbalance. But Jesus loves balance even more than Satan hates it. As we follow Jesus, he moves to strike his balance in our walk and maintain it in all our dealings with people.

The woman thrown at the feet of the Master Musician encountered acceptance, forgiveness, and change—a harmonious alternative to the squawking dissonance of her pain and brokenness. The Master Conductor played for her a balanced symphony of compassion and correction. This is what we get when life's music is played from the solid center.

Creative Touch

Help the guilty by creatively balancing truth and mercy.

Thought Questions

1. What is spiritual balance to you?

2. Describe a situation where you saw law applied in a way that may be harmful to people. Also one where you saw people viewed in a way that seemed to ignore sin.

3. Describe a situation where you, personally, may have misapplied God's word so that it hurt rather than helped the growth of God's people.

Action Questions

1. What steps can you take to achieve balance in your spiritual life?

2. What can you do to put Jesus' principles into practice this week in your church, your school, or at work?

3. How did Jesus offer the woman the correct balance of compassion with correction? In whose life can you offer the same?

Chapter 12

REPAIRING brokenness

WHEN HEAVEN'S FINGER TOUCHES HUMAN EARTHINESS

When the carpenter knelt for the second time and again began writing in the dirt, I closed my eyes and braced myself for the first stone to bite my flesh. A weird, tense silence fell over the crowd—except for the crunching of sandals on gravel.

Nothing happened.

Eternity passed, it seemed.

When the foot-shuffling died away, I finally opened my eyes. To my astonishment everyone had left but the carpenter. Again, he was looking at me.

When most men look at me, I feel naked, as if they are mentally undressing me. But never had I felt as bare as now. No, definitely not physically naked. This was no lustful leer. Oh, no. The compassion in the carpenter's eyes gently laid bare my soul. I thought I saw him blink back tears, and for the first time in forever—I felt decent.

Even though scant minutes earlier I had been inflamed with lust and then the crowd had been inflamed with hatred, still the carpenter looked at me—and at them—in this most unusual way. And all of us felt hope.

Jesus straightened up and asked her, "Woman, where are they? Has no one condemned you."

"No one, sir," she said.

"Then neither do I condemn you," Jesus declared. "Go now and leave your life of sin."

John 8:10–11

REPAIRING brokenness

WHEN HEAVEN'S FINGER TOUCHES HUMAN EARTHINESS

Did flying birds stop fluttering and turn curious heads downward? Did flowers crane necks upward to watch? Did squirrels on branches hold their breath and cup their ears to listen? Did heaven's angels cease singing and watch the carpenter rise from his feet and stand facing that woman? When the trembling woman opened her eyes, did she know that she was looking into the face of God?

How Jesus Touches Brokenness

It is doubtful that in his earthly ministry our Lord ever faced anyone as transparently vulnerable as was this lady at this moment. Caught in blatant sin. Publicly embarrassed. Terrified for her life. In debt to a stranger who had rescued her. She was totally at his mercy, not knowing what would happen next. Like a frightened bird that had fallen out of its nest, she must have quivered as she looked at the man who held her fate in his hands.

Have you ever stood in a place akin to Jesus' position at that moment? Times come when a person's dark secrets have been revealed to us, and a precious person stands before us—absolutely naked in failure. At times like these, we hold nearly absolute power over a broken soul.

It's not an easy place to be.

Someone pours his or her heart out to you, trusting you with intimate confessions. What do you say next? A friend hangs his or her head and admits cheating on a loving mate. What is your next step? You come home early one day to find your teenage daughter and her friends smoking pot in the garage. How do you respond? You, an elder in the church, sit across the table from the church treasurer who has been caught funneling church money into his or her business. How do you treat this person?

My longtime friend Carlos runs a prosperous business. People are naturally drawn to him because he is always a barrel of fun. Carlos also contagiously loves Jesus. In fact, his faith is so contagious that most people who come to work in his offices eventually receive Christ.

> HIS FAITH IS SO CONTAGIOUS THAT MOST PEOPLE WHO COME TO WORK IN HIS OFFICES EVENTUALLY RECEIVE CHRIST.

Jan, his bookkeeper, was one of those people. Some years back, Jan and her husband, Tom, who was not a believer, hit some rocky times in their marriage. The trouble revolved, as family trouble often does, around finances. They were in debt to their eyeballs.

One afternoon, Carlos was shocked to discover several thousand dollars missing from his business, covered by phony figures. At first he couldn't believe it was Jan. But the evidence left no other possibility.

I asked Carlos, "What did you do next?"

"Well," Carlos admitted, "first I closed the office door and cried. It really hurt me that it was Jan."

"And then…?"

Carlos told how he had called Jan in and confronted her. She didn't deny it for one second. She just began to cry and pour out her marital problems and financial crisis. She had given into temptation and "borrowed" the money, hoping against hope to replace it before it was found missing. She asked if Carlos had pressed charges yet and how soon she'd have to clear out her desk. But Carlos explained that there would be no charges. Besides, he said, she wasn't being fired. "You are my Christian sister, and I want to help you out of this mess," explained Carlos. "All I want is to know you are sorry, that it won't happen again, and that you'll pay the money back."

"But there is no way I can pay it back. We couldn't begin to borrow that much with our credit like it is," Jan said.

Carlos explained, "You can pay it back just a hundred dollars a month, till it's covered—at no interest."

Jan began to cry again, "But even that is impossible. Every penny is gone before I get my check."

"Sure you can, when you get your raise." Carlos explained, "Starting next week, I'm raising your salary by one hundred dollars a month."

"Why would you do that?"

"Because I don't want you crushed; I want to see you changed and happy and walking with Jesus."

Then Jan and Carlos prayed together. Jan continued working in Carlos's office as a trusted employee for years afterward and has been a loving follower of Jesus ever since.

I think Carlos learned this from Jesus, maybe from the exact point when Jesus stood facing the lady in John 8.

If ever a time calls for balance, a time like that does—a time when cheeks are stained by forbidden fruit. And perhaps it was for other times like this that the Holy Spirit recorded the final lines of Jesus' conversation with the woman caught in adultery.

Three World-Changing Words

When Jesus' dirt-writing finger came to a stop, he stood up, looked the woman in the eye, and spoke three messages. These three pivotal words changed her world and can change yours and mine as well.

A Word of Acceptance

First, Jesus asked, "Does no one condemn you?" These first words were words of *acceptance*. "No one threw any rocks at you? That means you aren't the only one who has stumbled." There is something wonderfully liberating in being reminded that "all have sinned and fall short of the glory of God" (Rom. 3:23).

Max Lucado said a friend saw this principle at work on a plane in a busy midwestern airport. The plane was full. The plane was late departing. The passengers were complaining. Not a good time to be a flight attendant, especially the one who caused the delay by forgetting to order the ice. Finally after an hour of sitting on the runway, a flight attendant stood before the planeload of disgruntled passengers and explained, "We apologize for the delay. We are late because one of your flight attendants forgot to order the ice for this flight. Because this airline frowns on such irresponsibility, the guilty employee will now stand before you."

The anger of the passengers melted into curiosity as they prepared to watch the public humiliation. This isn't something you see on every flight. You can imagine their surprise when the flight attendant turned, put up the microphone, then turned back and stood before the people. She was the culprit! She was the cause of the delay! Everyone sat a few seconds in stunned silence, not quite knowing how to react. Then a sensitive passenger began to clap his hands. Another followed suit. Soon everyone was applauding! The honest mistake was overshadowed by the honest confession.

Why did everyone applaud? Because each knew it could easily have been him or her. Everyone had forgotten important things a time or two. And for this hapless flight attendant, the applause was incredibly liberating; it was a reminder that she wasn't the only person who makes mistakes.

Jesus viewed the woman caught in adultery as a valued *person*. "Lady, don't you see that you're not alone? You're a human being. You're not a useless piece of garbage because you have sinned. You've probably felt isolated thinking you're the only woman in the world like this. That you must be some kind of freak. But they are all sinners too. Don't you see that nobody condemns you? You're not alone, lady. Not alone!" We are often helped out of our sin-traps when we simply learn that we're not alone. That we, like everyone else, are sinners in need of mercy!

A Word of Forgiveness

Jesus' next words were words of *forgiveness:* "Neither do I condemn you" (John 8:11). As long as I feel that God holds my sins against me, I cannot grow. But when I am convinced that God harbors no grudge, I can breathe the fresh air of new beginnings.

A woman once told her minister that Jesus came to visit her nightly before she went to bed. The minister was understandably skeptical. He questioned such favored treatment from heaven, but the woman insisted that it happened every night. So the preacher suggested a little test. "I committed a serious sin before entering the ministry. Ask Jesus tonight what that sin was and come back tomorrow with your answer. If you find out what the sin was, I will believe your story about personal visits from above."

Next day the dubious preacher asked. "Well, did you learn anything?"

"Yes. I asked him," the woman explained, "but he said he doesn't remember sins already forgiven."

The broken, humiliated woman who stood before Jesus didn't need to be reminded of her sins. She was painfully aware of them. What she needed was healing. She needed to be reminded that forgiveness was within arms' length and that with forgiveness comes forgetting.

James wrote an interesting prescription for the treatment and healing of sin: "Therefore confess your sins to each other and pray for each other so that you may be healed" (James 5:16).

What does the word *healed* presuppose? That a wound exists. The result of sin is a wound, a deep infected lesion that cannot be healed by the salt of accusation. It is healed only by the soothing balm of forgiveness. Jesus wanted her to get it out, get it over—and then to get on with life.

In other words, "You are forgiven too." What sweet-sounding words! I need those words often. We all do. We all harbor and hide our secrets, and at times, suffer alone. But this is so needless. For if we would just reach out for Jesus' healing touch, we could confess and be healed. His kind word for us can be, "I don't condemn you either. You're forgiven."

What if Jesus had said, "Well, I may not be smart, but I'm no dummy. If I'm going to continue my ministry, I obviously can't afford to alienate the power structure. The salvation of the whole world is at stake. It's a tough decision, ma'am. I understand that you've got a problem here, but, you see, you are only one person and my ministry is bigger than you. You're collateral damage, ma'am. Bring on the rocks, fellows. Sorry, lady."

> THE BROKEN, HUMILIATED WOMAN WHO STOOD BEFORE JESUS DIDN'T NEED TO BE REMINDED OF HER SINS. WHAT SHE NEEDED WAS HEALING.

A distorted sense of religiosity sometimes abuses individuals in the name of a broader ministry. I've seen it happen. You, too, right? Now, I realize that institutions can't play favorites. But God's ministry flourishes through redemptive relationships, not through right policy. In God's system of things, *people* are "job one." It is never right to do wrong to a person in the name of a larger good. Never.

Did I hear someone say, "Well, I realize that so-and-so is remorseful, but we've got to make an example of this case." That's not what Jesus did. When it comes to applying the law of God, we ought to lean the way Jesus leaned: toward mercy, not sacrifice. Mercy. God himself says that people are always more valuable than principles and institutions.

Jesus' creative principle here: *fight for people.* We are all infinitely precious to him and to our Father. Of course, Jesus was a person of principle. But he was even more willing to fight for people than to fight for principles. It is never right to do wrong by a person.

A Word of Change

The final words of Jesus to this woman spoke of *change.*

How creatively Jesus fought for her—and for those men. He offered *acceptance,* reminding her that she wasn't alone in her sins. He offered *forgiveness* and a fresh start. But now he *demands change.*

"Go now and leave your life of sin" (John 8:11). In saying this, Jesus was not trying to shore up the law or protect the system. On the contrary, he said it because he didn't want that woman to break herself. As Max Lucado says, "God loves us right where we are. But he loves us too much to leave us there." Adultery wrecks intimacy. Adultery smashes self-esteem. Adultery destroys trust. And adultery is not only *offensive* in the eyes of God; *it breaks his heart!*

To offer the woman compassion with no challenge to change her behavior would not have healed her brokenness. For while she was clearly a pawn in the Pharisees' power play, she was also a sinner. She had chosen to surrender to her own lust. A loving Jesus couldn't ignore that choice and whitewash her scarlet sin!

It is never loving to pretend that a sin didn't happen or that the sin doesn't matter. It was our sin that sent Jesus to his death!

What favor do we perform for wayward searching friends if we don't call them to change? What kind of physician stitches a wound but then offers no medication or therapy? Does love offer acceptance and forgiveness but no rescue? As Paul the Apostle put it, "Shall we go on sinning so that grace may increase? By no means!" (Rom. 6:1–2).

So Jesus' advice to the broken woman caught in adultery was clear and compelling. "Don't sin any more." In other words, "You are too valuable for that."

We don't know where this woman went from there. Scripture follows her no further. Some assume she became one of the faithful women who assisted Jesus in his ministry. Others imagine she was present at the cross. It is possible, however, that she didn't take Jesus' advice. She may even have gone right back into the sack from which she had been yanked. Who knows?

But we do know one thing for sure: She encountered a man who saw her pain and brokenness and offered her words of acceptance, forgiveness, and change.

Creative Touch

Fight for the personhood of wounded and broken people,
knowing that it is never right to do a person wrong.

Thought Questions

1. Describe a situation where you saw a dilemma between the need for compassionate forgiveness and the need for a person to change their ways.

2. Where is the healthy path between judgment and "cheap grace"?

3. Analyze this: "God loves you just where you are, but he loves you too much to leave you there."

Action Questions

1. What specific sin must you personally leave behind so that you, a forgiven person, can offer God a changed life? When will you do it?

2. What person do you know and love who needs to hear, "Your sins are forgiven: Go and sin no more"?

3. How can you communicate this to them lovingly and effectively? When will you do it?

Chapter 13

BEWARE OF pigeonholes
OF LABELS AND LIBELS

Oh, no! Not this again. It's bad enough not being able
to see. Why do some people have to humiliate blind
people just for sport? Like, last week, some kids dumped
the coins from my cup into the sand. When I bent down to
scratch around and find them, the kids kicked dirt in my
face and ran off laughing.

And the loud-talkers. They seem to think that blind
people are also deaf. They shout their greetings in my ear.
Others say the most painful things, right out loud. Like
the woman yesterday who stood right there and complained to her husband that the stuff running from my eye
sockets turned her stomach.

So, naturally, I was suspicious when this gang of men
walked up. I heard them ask the old questions again, right
in front of me, as if I had no more feelings than a rock or a
tree. "Is it his sin or that of his parents that took his
sight?"

The unusual note in his voice encouraged me. I felt
he was giving me dignity. And he said something about
God. But then he did the most confusing thing. I can hear
really small noises, you know. So I heard the creak of his

sandals and the rustle of his cloak as he knelt down. I could hear his fingers scratching around in the dirt. The rustle again as he stood. Then I heard him hock saliva from his throat and spit it in his palm. Next I was sure I could hear a squishy sound, like he was making spit-mud in his hand.

Then came the shock. Splat. He smacked his handful of spit-mud right in one of my eyes. This had to be the dirtiest trick anyone had pulled on me yet. I didn't know what to do. I wanted to run. But I held my ground, hoping they would leave. Then he repeated the process—splat—in my other eye!

Double insult. Finally he ordered, "Go wash your face in the pool!"

Here was my chance to exit! So I picked up my stick and tapped off in the direction of Siloam. When I felt my stick stir a splash, I fell on my knees and scooped handfuls of water onto my face and into my eyes until I heard my tormenters leave.

But then, when I stood up, for the first time in my life I saw light. Then trees. Water. Sky. Birds. Flowers.

I dropped my stick and ran for home...and chaos!

As he went along, he saw a man blind from birth. His disciples asked him, "Rabbi, who sinned, this man or his parents, that he was born blind?"

"Neither this man nor his parents sinned," said Jesus, "but this happened so that the work of God might be displayed in his life. As long as it is day, we must do the work of him who sent me. Night is coming, when no one can work. While I am in the world, I am the light of the world."

Having said this, he spit on the ground, made some mud with the saliva, and put it on the man's eyes. "Go," he told him, "wash in the Pool of Siloam" (this word means Sent). So the man went and washed, and came home seeing.

John 9:1–7

BEWARE OF pigeonholes
OF LABELS AND LIBELS

One of our sons-in-law, Wes, makes his living with music. Has most of his adult life. He and our daughter Michele moved to Colorado Springs on their wedding day nineteen years ago. They both love the mountains, and Wes had bookings in that area. They quickly found an apartment and left a résumé, a check, and a verbal agreement. But when they called back to pick up a key, the manager backpedaled, "Well, I'm having second thoughts. I noticed that you are a musician. Sorry, but we can't accept your application because our company caters to the more stable type of tenant."

Wes is an unusually even-tempered guy, but that got him steamed. He's never left an unpaid bill. He doesn't drink. He doesn't smoke. He doesn't like loud music. He doesn't throw wild parties. And he especially doesn't like being labeled unstable because he is a musician.

Actually, Wes is like all the rest of us. We like to be who we are. We want to be treated like people, not like categories.

One time a young attorney came to Jesus and said, "Could you help me sort out some issues of the law? What are the biggies?"

Jesus said, "Well, I'll explain that very simply. No use to be confused. The biggest issue is that you love God with all of your heart and your soul and your mind and your strength."

Someone says, "That all sounds fine, but I can't get a handle on that. For me, God is some sort of oblong blur on the fringe of my imagination. What does it mean to love God?"

Jesus came straight to the point. "To love God is to love your neighbors as yourself." Jesus' whole life demonstrated that. To love our neighbor is to be *available, sensitive, helpful,* and delightfully *creative* in the way we touch them—realizing that each person is unique and that God-given uniqueness is to be profoundly respected.

That's what Jesus said. Now watch him do it as he encounters a unique person in the ninth chapter of John. "As he went along, he saw a man blind from birth" (John 9:1); that's availability. Jesus gave him sight; that's helpfulness. And, putting spit-mud in the man's eyes is a most creative way to heal blindness. When the man went to the pool and washed the mud out of his eyes, he could instantly see!

They Could Not See What They Would Not See

But the healing of this blind man triggered a barrage of reactions from every direction. The disciples of Jesus didn't understand nor did the blind man's family and neighbors. And the Pharisees most definitely had some questions. The whole event created such uproar that the poor fellow was kicked out of his own church.

The biggest blindness, however, was in the minds of the people who raised questions about the man whom Jesus healed. They couldn't see the man, the human being who was given eyesight. They only saw a label. What is worse, they could not see that they would not see. But as we trace Jesus' walk through this whole scenario, we'll learn some creative people skills.

Five different groups of people viewed this blind man from five different perspectives.

The Disciples Saw a Question

The disciples asked Jesus a *religious* question: "Rabbi, who sinned, this man or his parents, that he was born blind?" (John 9:2). A logical question, given their times. For centuries, traditions had said that people were struck by catastrophe because of sin, either their own or their parents'. When a person suffered, they simply got what they had coming. Hence, the disciples' question: "Is this man blind because of his own sins or the sin of his parents?"

The disciples saw only a religious question. They did not see the person. What a convenient way to dismiss personhood: quite creative when you stop and think about it. Just head off into a world of abstractions, and you never

> TO LOVE OUR NEIGHBOR IS TO BE *AVAILABLE, SENSITIVE, HELPFUL,* AND DELIGHTFULLY *CREATIVE.*

have to actually deal with real human beings. And you might feel good about it, too, because the abstractions are *religious.* So while the abstract religion discussion continued, the blind man's feelings were ignored.

I saw something like this happen in our church. A person who had undergone a sex-change operation years earlier began attending services. No one in our church knew the person's secret past, probably still don't. One Sunday, while this person sat in Bible class, the group launched into a lively debate about sex-change surgery and Christian ethics. Let me tell you, if you want a topic that will occupy religious people for a while, that question has infinite possibilities. Why, you can cite experts on surgery, on sex, on morality, on theology, even on psychology. You can analyze the issue from now till judgment morning. You could even prepare a seminar on "Sex-Change and the Christian" and hit the speakers' circuit—without ever knowing a real live person who has had sex-change surgery, without ever offering Christ's compassion to such a person. I listened and watched that Sunday morning, as the sex-changed person felt like a "thing"—no, more like a category, an abstract religious question.

Not Jesus' way, however. For Jesus, any route that leads away from people eventually leads away from God. Mark that down!

I recall another occasion, sitting in the office with our church staff, heatedly discussing whether or not Christians should attempt to help "druggies" while they were actually stoned. Then we walked out of the church building to find a teenage girl lying unconscious on the sidewalk in the hot sun. She was toxified on drugs, had passed out, and was nearly dead—right in front of the church—while we had moments ago sat exploring drug abusers as abstract religious questions!

The Neighbors Saw a Category

The blind man's neighbors took another nonhuman view. They saw a *label*. "Isn't this the *beggar?*" To them he was not a person but "the beggar." Someone has said, "Labels are libels."

"He's a musician! Not in our apartment!" Labeling smoothly and conveniently distances us from involvement and with one word

232

dehumanizes the labeled person. Yet, paradoxically, at the time we slap on the label, we may even feel that we have "handled" the situation because we have defined which category he or she belongs in.

"Oh, Tom? He's an alcoholic."

Excuse me. I'm sorry. I treated him as if he was a person.

"See that guy over there? He's gay."

So? Should that change my basic way of treating him? Because his sin is homosexuality, does that make him less than a person?

"Susan? You know, she's a hooker."

Oh, I thought she was a human being. Maybe we need to get closer to Susan, a person who matters to God; maybe we should love her with Christ's love.

"Jim is radical, right-wing, ultra-conservative (or was it left-wing, ultra-liberal?)."

"Sarah is a divorcée!" (We usually don't say that a person was divorced or has been divorced or even was formerly married. It's easier to say "divorcée.")

One "Christian," door-knocking crusade leader instructed each door-knocker, "As soon as possible, find out if the person in that home is a divorcée. If so, exit as quickly and gracefully as you can, and go talk to somebody who is not damaged goods!" No, "damaged goods" was not the exact wording, but it was the clear meaning. Can you imagine Jesus reacting to the Samaritan woman that way? "Oh, my goodness. Well, I'd better exit this conversation ASAP. Maybe there's another well down the road with a better woman sitting by it. Can't waste any more time here."

Labeling seems to come so naturally, maybe especially for religious people. Bam, stick on the label! Cover up the person. Sidestep involvement and relationship, and scoot on down to the church.

The Pharisees Saw a Problem

The Pharisees viewed the blind man from a third perspective. "Now the day on which Jesus had made the mud and opened the man's eyes was a Sabbath" (John 9:14). Bingo! Sabbath! First clue something's gone wrong.

"Tell us how you received your sight."

"[Jesus] put mud on my eyes, and I washed, and now I see" (v. 15).

"Aha! We've got a problem here. This healer is not from God, or he wouldn't do this on the Sabbath."

The Pharisees saw a *problem* rather than a person.

"We've got to discredit this 'healer' of blind men. If our people go off after him, we'll lose our power. We'll have problems. We've got to keep our religious forum at all costs. Sure, we'll have to dump this blind man out of the church, but our forum has been around a lot longer than this guy has. We can't sacrifice it for him."

> THE PHARISEES SAW A *PROBLEM* RATHER THAN A PERSON!

The Pharisees had ignored the big question Jesus asked on a previous occasion when he had been criticized for Sabbath-day healing: "Which is lawful on the Sabbath: to do good or to do evil, to save life or to destroy it?" (Luke 6:9).

They hadn't responded. No point! They weren't really interested in the Sabbath law or in doing good. All they wanted was to protect their power at whatever cost, even if the cost was *people*. In Jesus' day or ours, whenever religious institutional force is used to crush human beings, God's purposes are prostituted.

We as God's people simply must not allow any institutional or political agenda to distract us from Christlike respect and compassion for individual people. When we abuse people for *any* reason, we're doing dreadful wrong. But what could be more destructive, evil, and damaging to the very nerve center of our character and our faith than toxic religion, which downgrades the value and meaning of people—in the name of God!

The Parents Saw a Family Role

A fourth take on this blind man came from his parents.

They were frightened. People routinely got kicked out of the synagogue for crossing swords with the leaders. And a sure way to offend the leaders was to admit interest in Jesus.

"Is this your son?" the leaders asked. "How is it that he can now see?"

"Son? Yes, that's our son, all right. Yes, he was born blind and can now see! But, understand, we have no idea how it was done!"

The parents' response was self-protective. Distortions of truth usually are. "This is our son. Our biological offspring." But the word *son* holds no warmth here. They saw their son as holding a position in their family; they didn't see an autonomous, precious person.

"She's just my wife."

"Only my husband"—the domestic partner.

God pity the son and daughter whose parents resent them, pay no attention to them, and see them only as their "kids." And heartbreak may be ahead for the mother or father whose children see them as just "my old man" and "my old lady." Respect is definitely on the way out of a marriage when a spouse sneers, "Oh, that's only my husband (or my wife) talking." This domestic discounting comes so easily and so inadvertently toward the people closest to us. Believe me, I know. I've done it!

235

Jesus Saw a Whole Person

Finally, let's look at this man through the eyes of Jesus. Go back and pick up the story at the beginning. Jesus *"saw a man blind from birth."* That's sensitivity. A world of loneliness and helplessness is packed into that phrase! Each word carries special poignancy. Saw! Saw a person! A blind person! Blind all of his life!

The disciples, neighbors, Pharisees, and family didn't really see. They did not discern who the blind man really was. They were looking only to their own concerns. But Jesus saw. What is more, he saw a man. He knew that he was in touch with a human being. He did not see a question or a problem or a label or a family role. He saw a *person.*

Even today blind people are sometimes dehumanized by their fellow humans, but much more so in Jesus' day. They were left to beg on the roadside. They were avoided. Ridiculed. Ostracized as a sure sinner under a curse! But Jesus saw a person. He understood the indignities experienced by a blind person in that ancient world. He knew they were cut off socially and regarded as morally and spiritually inferior. He understood the severity of suffering the indignities of blindness *all of his life!*

But beyond the human predicament, Jesus saw an opportunity for God. He said, "This happened so that the work of God might be displayed in his life."

Every human life holds magnificent potential to reveal God's glory. An old TV commercial comes to mind: A little boy is staring hungrily into a bakery window. He is wearing ragged clothes and has no money. "Mean Joe Green," a former Pittsburgh Steeler football pro-bowler, spots the little guy, edges up alongside him, and asks, "Do you like those doughnuts?"

"Yeah."

The little boy doesn't know "Mean Joe." Doesn't even look at him. Joe goes inside while the little boy's nose is pressed against the window. When Joe Green comes out, he stuffs a sack full of hot doughnuts into the little fellow's arms. As the scene fades the little guy looks toward the camera and asks, "Was that man God?"

Jesus said, "As long as it is day, we must do the work of him who sent me" (John 9:4). How? What does it mean to do the work of God? Mostly it means treating people like God treats people. We are meant to reflect the gentleness of God, the kindness of God, the goodness of God, the mercy, the patience, the joy, the peace, the courage, and the sensitivity of God. And we are meant to be creatively personal—like God. Then the work of God is being done through us! Then people can see God in us!

Sometimes I become so task-oriented that I make too little time for people. I rationalize to myself that the task is "the work of God." But God's most important work is *people.* Of course, some tasks that keep us away from people for a time actually are *for* people in the longer and larger picture. The point is, when we're doing right by people, we're doing the work of God—in the office, at home, down at the service station, at the gym. When God's work enriches our relationships, *folks see God.*

Several years ago in Arkansas, a non-churchgoing lady was befriended by some people in a small-town church. It happened when her baby fell sick with a life-threatening illness that lasted for weeks. People from that church pulled alongside her. They cleaned her house, put food in the refrigerator, and even helped pay the medical bills. Most importantly, they took turns holding the baby, day and night, around the clock until the baby was well. Eventually, the lady began attending that church. Her unchurched friends asked, "Are you going to church somewhere?"

"Yes, I've been going with the people over here."

"Oh, watch out for churches," the friends scoffed. "They are full of goody-goodies. They only want your money. They say that nobody is going to heaven but them."

The lady responded, "I've never heard them say that. They have never asked me for money. And I've been over there for weeks. I only know that when I thought my baby was dying, *they held my baby.*"

Her words resonate with the words of the blind man: "I don't know who he was; I just know that *I was blind, and now I can see.*" The world's most profound and eloquent preaching can't touch people nearly so deeply as the love of God in human skin.

When the blind man was healed, the watching crowd saw a religious question, a label, a problem, and a family role. But none of them saw a person. And they certainly didn't see "an instrument of God's glory." Only Jesus saw the *man.* And only Jesus saw God at work!

John wrote, "Dear friends, let us love one another, for love comes from God." John said that although no human eye will physically see God, "if we love one another, God lives in us and his love is made complete in us" (1 John 4:7, 12). When we treat people like God would treat then, those with eyes to see can see God. That's how folks see God, not merely by listening to religious talk.

Jesus Breaks the Darkness

Let's walk through the story one more time, this time in the blind man's shoes.

The man stands on the street corner, begging. Several strangers walk up and begin to discuss his plight—as if he were not even there to hear them. He wants to say, "Oh, go on, don't bug me. Don't humiliate me more. Don't steal my pencils or take the money out of my cup. Just keep walking if you have nothing to give me."

Then one of the strangers does something bizarre and gross. He rubs spit-mud onto the man's eyes and tells him to go to the pool to wash.

The blind man endures the spit. Splat! He was probably steeled against this kind of thing. He had had a lot of dirty tricks played on him through the years. So he heads for the pool and splashes water on his eyes. But wait! Something's changed. "Hallelujah, I can see!"

"I JUST KNOW THAT I WAS BLIND, AND NOW I CAN SEE."

Let's move further into the blind man's psyche. Upon reflection, one thing he could see was that Jesus had focused not on his own agenda (Kingdom priorities) but on the blind man's need (sight). I really need to learn that. Our human tendency in "witnessing" to others is to make people beholden to us, to hook them so we can conform them to our own agenda. But Jesus was neither pushy nor manipulative. He just met the man's needs. Then he backed off to give the man space. None of us likes to be shoved into things, even good things.

A Gentle Touch

J. Wallace Hamilton tells about a soldier who spotted a blind man being jostled by the crowd at the airport. The blind man had dropped his white cane and was fumbling to retrieve it so he could cross to another part of the terminal. The soldier stopped and offered, "Sir, can I help you?" The blind man beamed his appreciation. "Yessir, just need a little help crossing the street." The soldier was nearly late for his flight, but he picked up the cane and put it in the blind man's hand. He then grabbed the man's arm and hurriedly shoved him along toward the far curb. The poor fellow stumbled a while trying to match the soldier's pace, then shrugged the soldier loose and protested, "Don't push me, man. Don't possess me! I just need your touch on my shoulder to guide me where I'm going."

Jesus was gentle with his touch on the blind man in the Bible. And Jesus still doesn't shove people around to guarantee results today. Nor should we. He calls us to move with him into the lives around us the way he moved into the world of the blind man.

Of course, for the blind man, as for all of us, the central need was for God. That is the need Jesus aimed to meet. But Jesus chose good timing. He didn't open the conversation with the central need. First off, Jesus met the man's *felt* need: He simply gave him sight.

Remember: The reason this man was blind was so "the works of God could be made known." When human need is met in such a way, the work of God is begun, and things begin changing inside a person. Things began to happen inside the blind man, too, but he had to deal with those things by himself—and that took time with no pressure.

So Jesus sent the man to the pool where he would find sight—and then left! He left so unobtrusively that the Bible doesn't even notice Jesus' absence till later on. Sometimes what people need from us, their "helpers," is that we disappear, that we get lost!

We can be available without breathing down people's necks and smothering them. Sometimes we need to back off and give people space for reflection on what we've said or done, though we still stay in touch. People often need an assimilation period. The blind man did! So do folks today.

No Strings Attached

What Jesus did was unique. It would be reasonably safe to say that not one person in a hundred thousand experiences something being done for him or her with absolutely *no strings attached!*

Jesus just healed and hurried away. He left no calling card. He sent no bill. He took down no names; he collected no tips. He didn't even explain himself! That's pretty unique, isn't it?

When you stop and think about it, that's exactly what he does with us. No strings. He just meets our needs. Even when they put him on a cross, he didn't bargain, "Father, if you'll guarantee me ten thousand converts in the first five years, I'll go through with this thing." No guarantees. He just died—that's all.

When most of us help people, there are strings! Of course, we attempt to hide them, even from ourselves. But we usually expect something out of it. At the very least, we want to make them feel obligated to listen when we begin to witness to them. And we want some results for our efforts. But people aren't stupid, especially people who have lived a long time in the darkness, being misused and manipulated and pushed around by nearly everybody. People can feel a string a mile off, even if it's only a psychological string. They can smell it coming; we all expect strings.

My friend Landon Saunders tells of a conversation overheard in the ladies' room during break at one of his outreach seminars. "What's the catch here? Do you suppose these things he's giving away are really free?" Another lady said, "I think I've got it figured out. They are free to us, but he's going to ask us to sell them to our neighbors." They expected strings, couldn't believe anything could really be free.

To treat people like Jesus treated people is to help with no strings attached. When a person is genuinely treated like God would treat him or her, the action won't go ignored. It is planted into the person's system. Once there, although it may have a long gestation period, it is still working.

WHEN SUCH TESTING COMES, NO ONE CAN HELP US ESCAPE IT.

What Jesus did quietly but powerfully "worked on" the blind man. He had to deal with the internal processes going on inside his own soul. It was still working inside him when opposition tested him. "I can see again. I don't understand why it's upsetting the neighborhood so terribly. Why, even the friends of this healer are asking critical, insensitive questions. And my parents are scared to death. But, on the other hand, I sure do like seeing."

Time to Sort Things Out

The blind man needed space and time to process his experience. He had to struggle very personally and privately with the implications of it all. He needed to internalize his experiences, he needed to struggle inside his own soul with the implications of it all.

At first he may have wondered, "What's the catch? When does the other shoe fall? What does the healer want out of this?" But then he may have reflected further, "But I can *see!* A blind man receiving his sight. That's pretty amazing. I can't ignore something this big!" He also had to assimilate the accusations of the Pharisees: "The Pharisees are saying this man is a sinner, but if that is true, how could he have healed me? Who is the man?"

When such testing comes, no one can help us escape it. Testing comes not only from people around us; the biggest testing comes in the naked loneliness of the soul. No one can shove us through it, like the soldier who tried to shove the blind man through the airport.

Though Jesus didn't shove this man, other people kept after him until he finally said, "He is a prophet" (John 9:17). At that, the Pharisees went ballistic!

"Prophet?!"

"Yes, I think he's a prophet."

The man is "thinking out loud," processing internal issues. A lot of us most effectively process the things churning in our minds and our hearts as we try to explain them to someone else. First the man explained who healed him. Then he wondered out loud, "I think Jesus might be a prophet."

Again the Pharisees summoned the man to come see them. A "summons" is serious stuff. I picture the Pharisees around a horse-shoe-shaped table with the man who had been blind on a chair in the middle. "Give glory to God," they demanded (v. 24). What do you do with that? Their demand only led the man to probe deeper into the implications of his amazing experience. Notice: During this debate, Jesus didn't sit at the man's elbow and pass him notes. He left the man alone.

The teachers of the law asserted further, "We know this man is a sinner" (John 9:24).

"All I know is that I used to be blind and now I can see."

Then they answered, "How did this 'healer' do this?" (Read: "Some kind of mumbo, jumbo? Black magic? Snake oil?")

"I've already told you once," he replied. "Why do you want to hear it *again?*"

The man's conviction had been edging slowly but surely toward the point of no return. He now approached ground zero! Decision time. And the questioners inadvertently pushed him toward that decision. But you don't hear Jesus whispering in the background, "Come on, come on, man, commit"—though the man may have been whispering it to himself.

Finally, the man who had been blind resolutely stepped across the line. I can almost hear him suck in a deep breath and blurt out, "Do you want to become disciples *too?*" By adding the word "too," he implied, "Like me! Yes. I am already a disciple!" Decision! The simple word "too" slammed the door on his past!

This was too much for the Pharisees. "You are this fellow's disciple? We're disciples of Moses. Who knows where this Jesus guy came from?"

Don't miss the next line. It is both salt in their wounds and nails in his coffin: "Well, that's remarkable. I thought you guys were theologians! Jesus opened my eyes! Yet you don't know where he's from? Come, come. What have you been teaching me in Sabbath school all these years? You taught me that God doesn't listen to sinners. Right? He only listens to the godly man. Now, nobody, but *nobody* has ever heard of opening the eyes of a man born blind. Why, gentlemen, if this man weren't from God, he could do nothing of this magnitude. You are the ones who taught me that!"

Retrace some steps on the pathway of this man's emerging commitment:

"I don't know."

"I think he's a prophet."

"I am his disciple."

"This man is from God."

When he turned their own logic against them, the Pharisees exploded! "You are steeped in sin. Your very blindness is the result of sin! Where do you get the nerve to lecture us on theology?" And when they had verbally unloaded on him, they threw him out of the synagogue.

What a turbulent day for this man! Absolutely amazing. Utterly confusing. That morning, his lifetime of darkness had exploded into the glory of sight. By noon, the world had gone crazy. By midafternoon, he landed on his head in the dust outside his home church, feeling like a quarterback sacked by a three-hundred-pound linebacker. Did he wonder, *Maybe being able to see isn't such a good thing after all?* But by now he's made his decision. "That's my story, and I'm sticking to it."

Jesus had given him space. He'd waited. He didn't breathe down this man's neck. Didn't harass him. He let him think things through for himself. Jesus respected the enormous struggle going on in the man's soul. Yet all the while, God had been drawing the man, gently tugging at his heart!

In a sixty-minute conversation with a stranger on an aircraft, we need not strain to swing the topic around to religion and press for a decision. Jesus wouldn't operate like that. He didn't Rolodex names for follow-up. When we treat people "Jesus style," we need not hurry them along to a full commitment all at once. God has stationed another messenger somewhere down the road to pick up where we leave off when the person comes to another level of readiness. God puts his witnesses where he wants them. We never serve uselessly. He uses each witness as he chooses. With each encounter, his Spirit probes a little deeper into that heart. God is drawing, still. Some people you witness to will respond positively. But many won't. Not everyone responded positively to Jesus. That's worth remembering. Leaves us at peace.

Consolidating Gains

When he heard the man had been thrown out of the synagogue, Jesus found him and asked, "Do you believe in me?" Why did Jesus wait until now to ask this question? What if Jesus had pressed that question at his first encounter with the blind man? "Hey, Mr. Blind Man? Can you hear me? I know you can't see. But can you hear me?"

"Yes, I can hear just fine."

"Okay, then listen up. You need to believe that I am the Messiah."

"It's my eyes, man, my eyes. Do you know what it's like to be blind? It's my eyes, 'Messiah.' If you want to help me, help me where I hurt, help me *see.*"

But of course, that's not how Jesus began. He began precisely with the eyes. Jesus gave the man sight, then backed off to give him space, dignity, and personhood.

After the man had processed the implications of all that had happened to him, Jesus stepped back into the picture. Now the man was ready for the big question: "Do you believe in the Messiah?"

"Who is he, sir, so that I can believe in him?" Remember, this man had never seen Jesus before. On his last encounter with Jesus, the man had been blind. So, of course, he does not recognize Jesus by sight. It apparently has not occurred to him that he is actually standing face to face with the Messiah! Even as I write these words, I feel goose bumps up my spine. A magnificent moment! Angels must have held their breath and leaned in close. Jesus quietly identified himself, "The Messiah is talking to you right now."

Wham!

Suddenly, everything fits. The man shouted out, "I believe!" And he worshiped Jesus. The angels must have burst into a chorus of "hallelujahs"! This man had finally arrived at his moment of full commitment—through an internal process that had begun with no-strings-attached service.

Today, as well, Jesus commissions us to touch people the same way. Discern needs. Do what we can. Then back off. But don't go too far away. Watch with loving eyes as God works in them. Pray. Wait. Then be there when the time is right for the next step toward God.

13

Creative Touch

Learn to see individual human beings not as categories
to be manipulated but as people to serve unconditionally—
no strings attached.

Thought Questions

1. Describe a time when you got labeled. How did it feel?

2. What do you think tempts us to label people?

3. Describe a time when you felt pushed. How did it feel?

4. What do you think tempts us to push other people?

Action Questions

1. What are some ways you can overcome labeling in your church? How can you begin?

2. How can you witness with passion yet restrain the temptation to push?

3. Is there anyone you have labeled or pushed to whom you need to apologize? How? When?

EPILOGUE

One of my mentors, E. H. Ijams, lived more than ninety years and died nearly three decades ago. I still vividly remember him telling of a special Sunday afternoon when he was a young man in Nashville, Tennessee. He had often been invited to speak to a congregation of African Americans in the inner city. They met Sunday afternoons because that was a time when the white church "allowed coloreds" to use their building.

"One afternoon," E. H. Ijams recalled, "I stood and read in my text, 'Have this mind among yourselves that you have in Christ Jesus.' As I laid my Bible aside and drew a breath to begin the message, a little boy sitting near the back began singing, softly at first, and in a timid, thin voice, 'I wanna be like Jesus, in my heart.' Soon another voice chimed in, 'wanna be like Jesus in my heart.' Then one by one, voices joined the chorus, till every person in the room was singing in full voice, *I wanna be like Jesus in my heart.'* That column of song was so thunderously exuberant that it seemed even that old building shook and throbbed. 'I wanna be like Jesus...'"

That *is* what we really want, I think. To be like Jesus. Available to people, like Jesus was. Sensitive to people. Helpful. And creative, in how we deal with people—a creativity that matches the uniqueness of each person God is pleased to touch through us.

"Be like Jesus in my heart." Yes!

NOTES

Introduction: What? Me, Insensitive?

1. Stephen Covey, *Principle-Centered Leadership* tape series (Provo, Utah: Covey Leadership Center, 1997).

Chapter 2: The Wine Of Kindness

1. Quoted from Alan Loy McGinnis, *The Friendship Factor* (Minneapolis: Augsburg, 1979), 15.

2. William Barclay, *The Gospel of John,* Daily Bible Study series (Philadelphia: Westminster, 1955), 81–82.

Chapter 4: A Tale of Two Cities

1. George Barna, *The Frog in the Kettle* (Ventura, Calif: Regal Books, 1990), 117, 119.

2. Jim Dethmer, "The Unchurched: Understanding Them to Reach Them," *The Pastor's Update,* April 1992.

Chapter 5: The Abandoned Water Jar

1. Stephen B. Oates, *With Malice Toward None* (New York: Harper & Row, 1997), 412.

Chapter 6: Places in the Heart

1. Calvin Miller, *The Singer,* © 1975 Inter-Varsity Christian Fellowship of USA. Used by permission of Inter-Varsity Press, P. O. Box 1400, Downer's Grove, Ill. 60515.

Chapter 7: Kicking the Habit

1. George MacLeod, *Only One Way Left* (Glasgow: The Iona Community, 1956), 38.

Chapter 8: Do You Want to Get Well?

1. William Glasser, *Reality Therapy* (New York: Harper & Row, 1965), 93–94.

2. Roger S. Greenway and Timothy M. Monsma, *Cities: Mission's New Frontier* (Grand Rapids: Baker Books, 1989), 51, 53.

3. Viktor E. Frankl, *Man's Search for Meaning,* revised and updated, trans. Ilse Lasch (Boston: Washington Square Press, 1959), 12.

4. Sandra D. Wilson, *Released from Shame: Recovery for Adult Children of Dysfunctional Families* (Downer's Grove, Ill.: Inter-Varsity Press, 1990), 154.

Chapter 9: Different Strokes

1. Bill Hybels, *Discovering How God Wired You Up: Part #1, Temperament,* audiotape (Barrington, Ill.: Willow Creek Resources).

Chapter 10: The Jesus Style

1. Don McLeese, review of *Dino: Living High in the Dirty Business of Dreams,* by Nick Tosches, *Dallas Morning News,* 1 September 1992, 3.

2. Paul Burka, "Honesty Is the Best Politics," *Texas Monthly,* 1 November 1992, 3.

3. James E. Dittes, *When the People Say No* (New York: Harper & Row, 1979), 2, 4–5.